Prayer
Power

Prayer Power

Andrew Murray

Whitaker House

All Scripture quotations are taken from the *King James Version* (KJV) of the Holy Bible.

PRAYER POWER

Andrew Murray
ISBN: 0-88368-567-1
Printed in the United States of America
Copyright © 1998 by Whitaker House

Whitaker House
30 Hunt Valley Circle
New Kensington, PA 15068

Library of Congress Cataloging-in-Publication Data

Murray, Andrew, 1828–1917.
    [Prayer life]
    Prayer power / Andrew Murray.
       p.   cm.
    Originally published: The prayer life. Springdale, Pa. : Whitaker House, 1981.
    ISBN 0-88368-567-1
    1. Prayer—Christianity. I. Title.
BV210.2.M835   1998
248.3'2—dc21   98-43717

CONTENTS

Preface

A few words with regard to the origin of this book and the object with which it was written will help to put the reader into the right position for understanding its teaching. It was the outcome of a conference of ministers at Stellenbosch, South Africa, April 11–14, 1912. The occasion of the conference was as follows: Professor de Vos of our theological seminary had written a letter to the ministers of our church (Dutch Reformed Church) concerning the low state of spiritual life which marked the church universal generally, which, he said, ought to lead to the inquiry as to how far that statement included our church too. What had been said in the book *The State of the Church* called for deep searching of heart. He thought there could be no doubt about the truth of the statement in regard to the lack of spiritual power. He asked whether it was not time for us to come together and in God's presence to find out what might be the cause of the evil. He wrote: "If only we study the conditions in all sincerity, we shall have to acknowledge that our unbelief and sin are the cause of the lack of spiritual power; that this condition is one of sin and guilt before God, and nothing less than a direct grieving of God's Holy Spirit."

His invitation met with a hearty response. Our four theological professors, with more than two hundred ministers, missionaries, and theological students, came together with the above words as the keynote of our meeting. From the very first in the addresses there was the tone of confession as the only way to repentance and restoration. At a subsequent meeting the opportunity was given for testimony as to what might be the sins that made the life of the church so feeble. Some began to mention failings that they had seen in other ministers, either in conduct or in doctrine or in service. It was soon felt that this was not the right way; each must acknowledge that in which he himself was guilty.

The Lord graciously so ordered it that we were gradually led to the sin of prayerlessness as one of the deepest roots of the evil. No one could plead himself free from this. Nothing so reveals the defective spiritual life in minister and congregation as the lack of believing and unceasing prayer. Prayer is indeed the pulse of the spiritual life. It is the great means of bringing to the minister and people the blessing and power of heaven. Persevering and believing prayer means a strong and an abundant life.

When once the spirit of confession began to prevail, the question arose as to whether it would be indeed possible to expect to gain the victory over all that had in the past hindered our prayer lives. In smaller conferences held previously, it had been found that many were most anxious to make a new beginning, and yet they had not the courage to expect that they would be able to maintain that prayer life that they saw to be in accordance with the Word of God. They had often made the attempt but had failed. They did not dare to make any promise to the Lord to live and to pray as He would have them; they felt it was an impossibility for them.

Such confessions gradually led to the great truth that the only power for a new prayer life is to be found in an entirely new relationship to our blessed Savior. It is as we see in Him the Lord who saves us from sin—including the sin of prayerlessness—and our faith yields itself to a life of closer communion with Him, that a life in His love and fellowship will make prayer to Him the natural expression of our soul's life. Before we parted, many were able to testify that they were returning with new light and new hope to find in Jesus Christ strength for a new prayer life.

Many felt that this was only a beginning. Satan, who had so long prevailed in the inner chamber, would do his utmost with his temptations to make us yield once again to the power of the flesh and the world. Nothing but the teaching and the fellowship of Christ Himself could ever give the power to remain faithful.

The need was felt for some statement of the truths that had been dealt with at the conference, to remind those who had been present of what they had learned and of what would help them in the new endeavor after that prayer life that is so essential to a minister's success. It was also needed for those who had been prevented from coming and for the eldership in our church, who had in many cases felt the deepest interest in hearing what the purpose was for which their ministers had gone from home.

Early copies of the book were sent out with the thought that if the leaders of the church, ministers and elders, begin to see that in spiritual work everything depends upon prayer, and that God Himself is the helper of those who wait on Him, it would indeed be a day of hope for our church. It was at the same time meant for all believers who long for a life of more entire separation to the Lord. For all who desired to pray more and pray better, it sought to point them to the glory of God in the inner chamber, and the way in which that glory can rest upon the soul.

When first asked to have the book translated into English, I felt as if its composition had been too hurried and its tone, owing to the close connection with the meetings that had preceded, too colloquial to make this desirable. Further, my own limited strength made it impossible for me to think of rewriting it. When, however, my friend, Reverend W. M. Douglas, asked permission to translate it, I gave my consent. If God has a message through the book to any of His servants, I would count it a privilege to tell what He has done here in our church, as a suggestion of what He may do in other churches.

I close with my greetings to all the ministers of the Gospel and to the church members who may read these pages. I pray fervently that the grace of God would work among us conviction of sin, confession of deep need and helplessness, and then give the vision and the faith of what Jesus Christ can do for those who trust Him. May He give to more than one who reads, the courage to take counsel with his brothers and to seek for and obtain that full fellowship with God in prayer which is the very essence of the Christian life. It has been said: "It is only the prayerless who are too proud to own up to prayerlessness." Let us believe that there are many hearts waiting for the call inviting them to united and whole-hearted confession of shortcoming, as the only but the sure way of a return and restoration to God's favor, and the experience of what He will do in answer to prayer.

I wish to add one word more, in regard to "the Pentecostal prayer meetings" held throughout our church. These have had a very interesting and important place in our work. At the time of the great revival in America and Ireland in 1858 and following years, some of our elder ministers issued a circular urging the churches to pray that God might visit us also. In 1860, the revival broke out in various parishes. In April 1861, in one of our oldest congregations, there was very deep interest shown in prayer. During the week preceding Pentecost, the minister, who ordinarily preached only once on a Sunday, announced that in the afternoon there would be a public prayer meeting in the church. The occasion was one of extraordinary interest, and many hearts were deeply touched. As one result, the minister suggested that in the future the ten days between Ascension and Pentecost should be observed by daily prayer meetings. This took place the following year. The blessing then received was such that all the neighboring congregations took up the suggestion, and now for fifty years the ten days of prayer have been observed throughout the whole church.

Each year notes were issued as subjects of addresses and prayer. The result has been that throughout our whole church Christians have been educated in the knowledge of what God's Word teaches regarding the Holy Spirit, and have been stirred to seek and to yield themselves to His blessed leading.

These ten days have often proved the occasion for special effort with the unconverted, and of partial revival. And they have been the means of untold blessing in leading ministers and people to recognize the place that the Holy Spirit ought to have as the executive of the Godhead in the heart of the believer, in the dealing with souls, and in consecration to the service of the kingdom.

There is still very much indeed lacking of the full knowledge and power of the Holy Spirit, but we feel that we cannot be sufficiently grateful to God for what He has done through His leading us to dedicate these days to special prayer for the movings of His Holy Spirit.

I have written this with the thought that there may be some who will be glad to know of it, and in their sphere to unite in the observance.

ANDREW MURRAY

chapter 1

The Sin of Prayerlessness

I n order for the conscience to do its work and for the heart to be thoroughly repentant, each individual must mention his sin by name. The confession must be severely personal. With ministers there is probably no single sin that each one of us ought to acknowledge with deeper shame—"Guilty, verily guilty"—than the sin of prayerlessness.

What is it, then, that makes prayerlessness such a great sin? At first it is looked upon merely as a weakness. There is so much talk about lack of time and all sorts of distractions that the deep guilt of the situation is not recognized. Let it be our honest desire that, for the future, the sin of prayerlessness may be to us truly sinful. Consider the following.

1. What a reproach it is to God.

There is the holy and most glorious God who invites us to come to Him, to converse with Him, to ask from Him such things as we need, and to experience what a blessing there is in fellowship with Him. He has created us in His own image and has redeemed us by His own Son, so that when we are in prayer with Him, we might find our highest glory and salvation.

What use do we make of this heavenly privilege? How many there are who take only five minutes for prayer! They say that they have no time and that the heart desire for prayer is lacking; they do not know how to spend half an hour with God! It is not that they absolutely do not pray; they pray every day—but they have no joy in prayer, as a token of communion with God that shows that God is everything to them.

If a friend comes to visit them, they have time, they make time, even at the cost of sacrifice, for the sake of enjoying conversation with him. Yes, they have time for everything that really interests them, but no time to practice fellowship with God and delight themselves in Him! They find time for a creature who can be of service to them; but day after day, month after month passes, and there is no time to spend one hour with God.

Do not our hearts begin to acknowledge what a dishonor this is to God, that I dare to say I cannot find time for fellowship with Him? If this sin begins to appear plain to us, will we not with deep shame cry out: "*'Woe is me! for I am undone'* (Isaiah 6:5), O God, be merciful to me and forgive this awful sin of prayerlessness"?

2. The sin of prayerlessness is the cause of a deficient spiritual life.

It is a proof that, for the most part, our lives are still under the power of the flesh. Prayer is the pulse of life; by it the doctor can tell what is the condition of the heart. The sin of prayerlessness is a proof for the ordinary Christian or minister that the life of God in the soul is in deadly sickness and weakness.

Much is said and many complaints are made about the feebleness of the church to fulfill her calling, to exercise an influence over her members, to deliver them from the power of the world, and to bring them to a life of holy consecration to God. Much is also spoken about her indifference to the millions of heathen whom Christ entrusted to the church that she might make known to them His love and salvation.

What is the reason that many thousands of Christian workers in the world do not have a greater influence? Nothing except this—the prayerlessness of their service. In the midst of all their zeal in the study and in the work of the church, of all their faithfulness in preaching and conversation with the people, they lack that ceaseless prayer that has attached to it the sure promise of the Spirit and the *"power from on high"* (Luke 24:49).

Once again, it is nothing but the sin of prayerlessness that is the cause of the lack of powerful spiritual life!

3. The church suffers a dreadful loss as a result of prayerlessness of the minister.

The business of a minister is to train believers to a life of prayer, but how can a leader do this if he himself has little understanding of the art of conversing with God and of receiving from the Holy Spirit, every day, abundant grace for himself and for his work? A minister cannot lead a congregation higher than he is himself. He cannot with enthusiasm point out a way, or explain a work, in which he is not himself walking or living.

Many thousands of Christians know next to nothing of the blessedness of prayer fellowship with God! Many more know something of it and long for a further increase of this knowledge, but in the preaching of the Word they are not persistently urged to keep on until they obtain the blessing! The reason is simply and only that the minister understands so little about the secret of powerful prayer and does not give prayer the place in his service that, in the nature of the case and in the will of God, is indispensably necessary. What a difference we would notice in our congregations if ministers could be brought to see in its right light the sin of prayerlessness and were delivered from it!

4. With prayerlessness evident, it is impossible to preach the Gospel to all men.

To proclaim the Good News to the world—as we are commanded by Christ to do—is an utterly unattainable dream as long as this sin is not over-come and cast out.

Many feel that the great need of missions is the obtaining of men and women who will give themselves to the Lord to strive in prayer for the salvation of souls. It has also been said that God is eager and able to deliver and bless the world He has redeemed, if His people were but willing, if they were but ready, to cry to Him day and night. But how can congregations be brought to that un-less there comes first an entire change in ministers, that they begin to see that the indispensable thing is not preaching, not pastoral visitation, not church work, but fellowship with God in prayer until they are clothed with *"power from on high"* (Luke 24:49)?

Oh, that all thought and work and expecta-tion concerning the kingdom might drive us to the acknowledgment of the sin of prayerlessness! God help us to root it out! God deliver us from it through the blood and power of Christ Jesus! God teach every minister of the Word to see what a glo-rious place he may occupy if he first of all is deliv-ered from this root of evils; so that with courage and joy, in faith and perseverance, he can go on with his God!

The sin of prayerlessness! May the Lord lay the burden of it so heavy on our hearts that we cannot rest until it is taken far from us through the name and power of Jesus. He will make this possi-ble for us.

A WITNESS FROM AMERICA

In 1898, there were two members of the Presbytery in New York who attended the North-field Conference for the deepening of their spiritual lives. They returned to their work with the fire of a new enthusiasm. They endeavored to bring about a revival in the entire Presbytery. In a meeting that they held, the chairman was guided to ask the other believers a question concerning their prayer life: "Brothers," said he, "let us today make confession before God and each other. It will do us good. Will everyone who spends half an hour every day with God in connection with his work hold up a hand?" One hand was held up. He made a further request: "All who thus spend fifteen minutes hold up a hand." Not half of the hands were held up. Then he said, "Prayer, the working power of the church of Christ, and half of the workers make hardly any use of it! All who spend five minutes hold up a hand." All hands went up. But one man came later with the confession that he was not quite sure if he spent five minutes in prayer every day. "It is," said he, "a terrible revelation of how little time I spend with God."

THE CAUSE OF PRAYERLESSNESS

In an elder's prayer meeting, a brother asked the question: "What, then, is the cause of so much prayerlessness? Is it not unbelief?"

The answer was: "Certainly; but then comes the question—what is the cause of that unbelief?" When the disciples asked the Lord Jesus: *"Why could not we cast* [the Devil] *out?"* (Matthew 17:19), His answer was, *"Because of your unbelief"* (v. 20). He went further and said: *"Howbeit this kind goeth not out but by prayer and fasting"* (v. 21). If the life is not one of self-denial, of fasting—that is, letting the world go—of prayer—that is, laying hold of heaven—faith cannot be exercised. A life lived according to the flesh and not according to the Spirit—it is in this that we find the origin of the prayerlessness of which we complain. As we came out of the meeting, a brother said to me: "That is the whole difficulty; we wish to pray in the Spirit and at the same time walk after the flesh, and this is impossible."

If one is sick and desires healing, it is of prime importance that the true cause of the sickness be discovered. This is always the first step toward recovery. If the particular cause is not recognized, and attention is directed to subordinate causes, or to supposed but not real causes, healing is out of the question. In the same way, it is of the utmost importance for us to obtain a correct insight into the cause of the sad condition of deadness and failure in prayer in the inner chamber, which should be such a blessed place for us. Let us seek to realize fully what is the root of this evil.

Scripture teaches us that there are but two conditions possible for the Christian. One is a walk according to the Spirit, the other a walk according to the flesh. These two powers are in irreconcilable conflict with each other. So it comes to pass, in the case of the majority of Christians, that, while we thank God that they are born again through the Spirit and have received the life of God—yet their ordinary daily life is not lived according to the Spirit but according to the flesh. Paul wrote to the Galatians: *"Are ye so foolish? having begun in the Spirit, are ye now made perfect by the flesh?"* (Galatians 3:3). Their service lay in fleshly outward performances. They did not understand that where *"the flesh"* is permitted to influence their service for God, it soon results in open sin.

So he mentions not only grave sins as the work of the flesh, such as adultery, murder, drunkenness; but also the more ordinary sins of daily life—wrath, strife, variance—and he gives the exhortation: *"Walk in the Spirit, and ye shall not fulfil the lust of the flesh....If we live in the Spirit, let us also walk in the Spirit"* (Galatians 5:16, 25). The Spirit must be honored not only as the Author of a new life, but also as the Leader and Director of our entire walk. Otherwise we are what the apostle calls "carnal."

The majority of Christians have little understanding of this matter. They have no real knowledge of the deep sinfulness and godlessness of that carnal nature that belongs to them and to which unconsciously they yield. *"God...condemned sin in the flesh"* (Romans 8:3)—in the Cross of Christ.

22

"They that are Christ's have crucified the flesh with the affections and lusts" (Galatians 5:24). *"The flesh"* cannot be improved or sanctified. *"The carnal mind is enmity against God: for it is not subject to the law of God, neither indeed can be"* (Romans 8:7). There is no means of dealing with the flesh except as Christ dealt with it, bearing it to the cross. *"Our old man is crucified with him"* (Romans 6:6); so we by faith also crucify it, and regard and treat it daily as an accursed thing that finds its rightful place on the accursed cross.

It is saddening to consider how many Christians there are who seldom think or speak earnestly about the deep and immeasurable sinfulness of the flesh: *"In me (that is, in my flesh,) dwelleth no good thing"* (Romans 7:18). The man who truly believes this may well cry out: *"I see another law in my members...bringing me into captivity to the law of sin....O wretched man that I am! who shall deliver me from the body of this death?"* (vv. 23–24). Happy is he who can go further and say: *"I thank God through Jesus Christ our Lord....For the law of the Spirit of life in Christ Jesus hath made me free from the law of sin and death"* (Romans 7:25, 8:2).

Would that we might understand God's counsels of grace for us! The flesh on the cross—the Spirit in the heart and controlling the life.

This spiritual life is too little understood or sought after; yet it is literally what God has promised and will accomplish in those who unconditionally surrender themselves to Him for this purpose.

Here then we have the deep root of evil as the cause of a prayerless life. The flesh can say prayers well enough, calling itself religious for so doing and thus satisfying conscience. But the flesh has no desire or strength for the prayer that strives after an intimate knowledge of God, that rejoices in fellowship with Him, and that continues to lay hold of His strength. So, finally, it comes to this: the flesh must be denied and crucified.

The Christian who is still carnal has neither desire nor strength to follow after God. He rests satisfied with the prayer of habit or custom. But the glory, the blessedness of secret prayer is a hidden thing to him, until one day his eyes are opened, and he begins to see that the flesh, in its disposition to turn away from God, is the archenemy that makes powerful prayer impossible for him.

I had once, at a conference, spoken on the subject of prayer and made use of strong expressions about the enmity of the flesh as a cause of prayerlessness. After the address, the minister's wife said that she thought I had spoken too strongly. She was also guilty of having too little desire for prayer, but she believed her heart was sincerely set on seeking God. I showed her what the Word of God said about the flesh, and that everything that prevents the reception of the Spirit is nothing else than a secret work of the flesh. Adam was created to have fellowship with God and enjoyed it before his Fall. After the Fall, however, there came immediately a deepseated aversion to God, and he fled from Him. This incurable aversion is the characteristic of the unregenerate nature and the chief cause of our unwillingness to surrender ourselves to fellowship with God in prayer. The following day she told me that God had opened her eyes; she confessed that the enmity and unwillingness of the flesh was the hidden hindrance in her defective prayer life.

Oh, my fellow believers, do not seek to find in circumstances the explanation of this prayerlessness over which we mourn; seek it where God's Word declares it to be, in the hidden aversion of the heart to a holy God.

When a Christian does not yield entirely to the leading of the Spirit—and this is certainly the will of God and the work of His grace—he lives, without knowing it, under the power of the flesh. This life of the flesh manifests itself in many different ways. It appears in the hastiness of spirit, or the anger that so unexpectedly arises in you, or the lack of love for which you have so often blamed yourself. It also appears in the pleasure found in eating and drinking when your conscience chides you; in that seeking for your own will and honor, that confidence in your own wisdom and power, that pleasure in the world, of which you are sometimes ashamed before God. All this is life after the flesh. *"Ye are yet carnal"* (1 Corinthians 3:3)—that text, perhaps, disturbs you at times; you have not full peace and joy in God.

I pray that you will take time and give an answer to the question: Have I not found here the cause of my prayerlessness, of my powerlessness to effect any change in the matter? I live in the Spirit, I have been born again, but I do not walk after the Spirit—the flesh lords it over me. The carnal life cannot possibly pray in the spirit and power. God forgive me. The carnal life is evidently the cause of my sad and shameful prayerlessness.

THE STORM CENTER ON THE BATTLEFIELD

Mention was made in the conference of the expression "strategic position" used so often in reference to the great strife between the kingdom of heaven and the powers of darkness.

When a general chooses the place from which he intends to strike the enemy, he pays the most attention to those points that he thinks are the most important in the fight. Thus there was on the battlefield of Waterloo a farmhouse that Wellington immediately saw as the key to the situation. He did not spare his troops in his endeavor to hold that point; the victory depended on it. So he won the victory. It is the same in the conflict between the believer and the powers of darkness. The inner chamber is the place where the decisive victory is obtained.

The Enemy uses all his power to lead the Christian, and above all the minister, to neglect prayer. He knows that however admirable the sermon may be, however attractive the service appears, however faithful the pastoral visitation, none of these things can damage him or his kingdom if prayer is neglected. When the church shuts herself up to the power of the inner chamber, and the soldiers of the Lord have received on their knees *"power from on high"* (Luke 24:49), then the powers of darkness will be shaken and souls will be delivered. In the church, on the mission field, with the minister and his congregation, everything depends on the faithful exercise of the power of prayer.

In the week of the conference I found the following in *The Christian:*

> Two persons quarrel over a certain point.
> We call them Christian and Apollyon.
> Apollyon notices that Christian has a certain weapon that would give him a sure victory. They meet in deadly strife, and Apollyon resolves to take away the weapon from his opponent and destroy it. For the moment the main cause of the strife has become subordinate; the great point now is who will get possession of the weapon on which everything depends? It is of vital importance to get hold of that.

So it is in the conflict between Satan and the believer. God's child can conquer everything by prayer. Is it any wonder that Satan does his utmost to snatch that weapon from the Christian, or to hinder him in the use of it?

Now how does Satan hinder prayer? By temptation to postpone or curtail it, by bringing in wandering thoughts and all sorts of distractions, or through unbelief and hopelessness. Happy is the prayer hero who, through it all, takes care to hold fast and use his weapon. Like our Lord in Gethsemane, the more violently the Enemy attacked, the more earnestly He prayed and did not cease until He had obtained the victory. After all the other parts of the armor had been named, Paul added, *"With all prayer and supplication in the Spirit"* (Ephesians 6:18). Without prayer, the helmet of salvation, the shield of faith, and the sword of the Spirit, which is God's Word, have no power. All depends on prayer. May God teach us to believe this and to hold fast!

chapter 2

The Fight against Prayerlessness

As soon as the Christian becomes convinced of his sin in this matter, his first thought is that he must begin to strive, with God's help, to gain the victory over it. But alas, he soon experiences that his striving is worth little, and the discouraging thought comes over him, like a wave, that such a life is not for him—he cannot continue faithfully! At conferences on the subject of prayer, held during the past years, many a minister has openly said that it seemed impossible for him to attain such a strict life.

Recently, I received a letter from a minister, well-known for his ability and devotion, in which he wrote: "As far as I am concerned, it does not seem to help me to hear too much about the life of prayer, about the strenuous exertion for which we must prepare ourselves, and about all the time and trouble and endless effort it will cost us. These things discourage me; I have heard them so often. I have time after time put them to the test, and the result has always been sadly disappointing. It does not help me to be told: 'You must pray more, and hold a closer watch over yourself, and become altogether a more earnest Christian.'"

My reply to him was as follows: "I think in all I spoke at the conference or elsewhere, I have never mentioned exertion or struggle, because I am so entirely convinced that our efforts are futile unless we first learn how to abide in Christ by a simple faith."

My correspondent said further: "The message I need is this: 'See that your relationship to your living Savior is what it ought to be. Live in His presence, rejoice in His love, rest in Him.'"

A better message could not be given, if only it is rightly understood. "See that your relationship to the living Savior is what it ought to be." But this is just what will certainly make it possible for one to live the life of prayer.

We must not comfort ourselves with the thought of standing in a right relationship to the Lord Jesus while the sin of prayerlessness has power over us, and while we, along with the whole church, have to complain about our feeble lives that make us unfit to pray for ourselves, the church, or missions as we ought. But if we recognize that a right relationship to the Lord includes prayer, with both the desire and power to pray according to God's will, then we have something that gives us the right to rejoice in Him and to rest in Him.

I have related this incident to point out how discouragement will naturally be the result of self-effort and will shut out all hope of improvement or victory. And this indeed is the condition of many Christians when called on to persevere in prayer as intercessors. They feel it is something entirely beyond their reach. They believe that they do not have the power for the self-sacrifice and consecration necessary for such prayer. They shrink from the effort and struggle that will, as they suppose, make them unhappy. They have tried in the power of the flesh to conquer the flesh—a wholly impossible thing. They have endeavored by Beelzebub to cast out Beelzebub—this can never happen. It is Jesus alone who can subdue the flesh and the Devil.

We have spoken of a struggle that will certainly result in disappointment and discouragement. This is the effort made in our own strength. But there is another struggle that will certainly lead to victory. The Scripture speaks of *"the good fight of faith"* (1 Timothy 6:12), that is to say, a fight that springs from and is carried on by faith. We must get right conceptions about faith and stand fast in our faith. Jesus Christ is always the Author and Finisher of our faith (Hebrews 12:2). It is when we come into right relationship with Him that we can be sure of the help and power He bestows. Just as earnestly as we must, in the first place, say, "Do not strive in your own strength; cast yourself at the feet of the Lord Jesus, and wait upon Him in the sure confidence that He is with you and works in you"; so do we, in the second place, say, "Strive in prayer; let faith fill your heart; so will you be strong in the Lord and in the power of His might."

An illustration will help us to understand this. A devoted Christian woman who conducted a large Bible class with zeal and success came to see her minister quite troubled. In her earlier years she had enjoyed much blessing in the inner chamber, in fellowship with the Lord and His Word. But this had gradually been lost, and, do what she would, she could not get right. The Lord had blessed her work, but the joy had gone out of her life. The minister asked what she had done to regain the lost blessedness. "I have done everything," said she, "that I can think of, but all in vain."

He then questioned her about her experience in connection with her conversion. She gave an immediate and clear answer: "At first I spared no pains in my attempt to become better and to free myself from sin, but it was all useless. At last I began to understand that I must lay aside all my efforts, and simply trust the Lord Jesus to bestow on me His life and peace, and He did it."

"Why then," said the minister, "do you not try this again? As you go to your inner chamber, however cold and dark your heart may be, do not try in your own might to force yourself into the right attitude. Bow before Him, and tell Him that He sees in what a sad state you are and that your only hope is in Him. Trust Him with a childlike trust to have mercy upon you, and wait upon Him. In such a trust you are in a right relationship to Him. You have nothing; He has everything." Some time later she told the minister that his advice had helped her. She had learned that faith in the love of the Lord Jesus is the only method of getting into fellowship with God in prayer.

Do you begin to see, my reader, that there are two kinds of warfare—the first when we seek to conquer prayerlessness in our own strength? In that case, my advice to you is: "Give over your restlessness and effort; fall helpless at the feet of the Lord Jesus. He will speak the word, and your soul will live." If you have done this, then, second, comes the message: "This is but the beginning of everything. It will require deep earnestness and the exercise of all your power and a watchfulness of the entire heart—eager to detect the least backsliding. Above all, it will require a surrender to a life of self-sacrifice that God really desires to see in us and which He will work out for us."

chapter 3

How to Be Delivered from
Prayerlessness

The greatest stumbling block in the way of victory over prayerlessness is the secret feeling that we will never obtain the blessing of being delivered from it. We have often put forth effort in this direction, but in vain. Old habits and the power of the flesh, our surroundings with their attractions, have been too strong for us. What good is it to attempt that which our heart assures us is out of our reach? The change needed in the entire life is too great and too difficult. If the question is asked, "Is a change possible?" our sighing heart says, "Alas, for me it is entirely impossible!" Do you know why that reply comes? It is simply because you have received the call to prayer as the voice of Moses and as a command of the law. Moses and his law have never yet given anyone the power to obey.

Do you really long for the courage to believe that deliverance from a prayerless life is possible for you and may become a reality? Then you must learn the great lesson that such a deliverance is included in the redemption that is in Christ Jesus, that it is one of the blessings of the new covenant that God Himself will impart to you through Christ Jesus. As you begin to understand this, you will find that the exhortation, *"Pray without ceasing"* (1 Thessalonians 5:17) conveys a new meaning. Hope begins to spring up in your heart that the Spirit—who has been bestowed on you to cry constantly, *"Abba, Father"* (Galatians 4:6)—will make a true life of prayer possible for you. Then you will hearken, not in the spirit of discouragement, but in the gladness of hope, to the voice that calls you to repentance.

Many a one has turned to his inner chamber, under bitter self-accusation that he has prayed so little, and has resolved for the future to live in a different manner. Yet no blessing has come; there was not the strength to continue faithfully, and the call to repentance had no power, because his eyes had not been fixed on the Lord Jesus. If he had only understood, he would have said, "Lord, you see how cold and dark my heart is; I know that I must pray, but I feel I cannot do so. I lack the urgency and desire to pray."

He did not know that at that moment the Lord Jesus in His tender love was looking down upon him and saying: "You cannot pray; you feel that all is cold and dark: why not give yourself over into My hands? Only believe that I am ready to help you in prayer. I long greatly to shed My love abroad in your heart, so that you, in the consciousness of weakness, may confidently rely on Me to bestow the grace of prayer. Just as I will cleanse you from all other sins, so also will I deliver you from the sin of prayerlessness—only do not seek the victory in your own strength. Bow before Me as one who expects everything from his Savior. Let your soul keep silence before Me, however sad you feel your state to be. Be assured of this—I will teach you how to pray."

Many a person will acknowledge, "I see my mistake. I had not thought that the Lord Jesus must deliver and cleanse me from this sin also. I had not understood that He was with me every day in the inner chamber, in His great love ready to keep and bless me, however sinful and guilty I felt myself to be. I had not supposed that just as He will give all other graces in answer to prayer, so, above all and before all, He will bestow the grace of a praying heart. What folly to think that all other blessings must come from Him, but that prayer, on which everything else depends, must be obtained by personal effort!

"Thank God I begin to comprehend that the Lord Jesus is Himself in the inner chamber watching over me and holding Himself responsible to teach me how to approach the Father. He only demands this: that I, with childlike confidence, wait upon Him and glorify Him."

Brothers and sisters, have we not seriously forgotten this truth? From a defective spiritual life, nothing better can be expected than a defective prayer life. It is vain for us, with our defective spiritual life, to endeavor to pray more or better. It is an impossibility. Nothing less is necessary than that we should experience that he who is in Christ Jesus *"is a new creature: old things are passed away; behold, all things are become new"* (2 Corinthians 5:17). This is literally true for the man who understands and experiences what it is to be in Jesus Christ.

Our whole relationship to the Lord Jesus must be a new thing. I must believe in His infinite love, which really longs to have communion with me every moment and to keep me in the enjoyment of His fellowship. I must believe in His divine power, which has conquered sin and will truly keep me from it. I must believe in Him who, as the great Intercessor, through the Spirit, will inspire each member of His body with joy and power for communion with God in prayer. My prayer life must be brought entirely under the control of Christ and His love. Then, for the first time, will prayer become what it really is, the natural and joyous breathing of the spiritual life, by which the heavenly atmosphere is inhaled and then exhaled in prayer.

Do you not see that, just as this faith possesses us, the call to a life of prayer that pleases God will be a welcome call? The cry, "Repent of the sin of prayerlessness," will not be responded to by a sigh of helplessness or by the unwillingness of the flesh.

The voice of the Father will be heard as He sets before us a widely opened door and receives us into blessed fellowship with Himself. When we pray for the Spirit's help, it will no longer be in the fear that prayer is too great an effort for us. Instead, we will simply fall down at the Lord's feet in our weakness. There we will find the victory and power that comes from His love.

The question may arise in our minds: "Will this continue?" And with it the fear comes: "You know how often you have tried and been disappointed." But faith will find its strength, not in the thought of what you will or do, but in the unchanging faithfulness and love of Christ, who has assured you, once again, that those who wait on Him will not be ashamed.

If fear and hesitation still remain, I pray that by the mercies of God in the Lord Jesus Christ, and by the unspeakable faithfulness of His tender love, you dare to cast yourselves at His feet. Only believe with your whole heart that there is deliverance from the sin of prayerlessness.

"If we confess our sins, he is faithful and just to forgive us our sins, and to cleanse us from all unrighteousness" (1 John 1:9). In His blood and grace there is complete deliverance from all unrighteousness and from all prayerlessness. Praised may His name be forever!

HOW DELIVERANCE FROM PRAYERLESSNESS MAY CONTINUE

What we have said about deliverance from the sin of prayerlessness also applies to the question: "How may the experience of deliverance be maintained?" Redemption is not granted to us piecemeal or as something that we may make use of from time to time. It is bestowed as a fullness of grace stored up in the Lord Jesus, which may be enjoyed in a new fellowship with Him every day. It is so necessary that this great truth should be driven home and fastened in our minds that I will once more mention it. Nothing can preserve you from carelessness, or make it possible for you to persevere in living, powerful prayer, except a daily close fellowship with Jesus our Lord.

He said to His disciples: *"Ye believe in God, believe also in me....Believe me that I am in the Father, and the Father in me....He that believeth on me, the works that I do shall he do also; and greater works than these shall he do"* (John 14:1, 11–12). The Lord wished to teach His disciples that all they had learned from the Old Testament concerning the power and holiness and love of God must now be transferred to Him. They must not believe merely in certain written documents but in Him personally. They had to believe that He was in the Father, and the Father in Him, in such a sense that they had one life, one glory. All that they knew about Christ they would find in God. He laid much emphasis on this because it was only through such a faith in Him and His divine glory that they could do the works that He did, or even greater works. This faith would lead them to know that just as Christ and the Father are one, so also they were in Christ and Christ was in them.

It is this intimate, spiritual, personal, uninterrupted relationship to the Lord Jesus that manifests itself powerfully in our lives, and especially in our prayer lives. Let us consider this and see what it means: that all the glorious attributes of God are in our Lord Jesus Christ. Think of the following.

1. The omnipresence of God.

His presence fills the world and every moment is present in everything. Just as it is with the Father, so now our Lord Jesus is everywhere present, above all with each of His redeemed ones. This is one of the greatest and most important lessons that our faith must learn. We can clearly understand this from the example of our Lord's disciples. What was the special privilege of these disciples, who were always in fellowship with Him? It was uninterrupted enjoyment of the presence of the Lord Jesus. It was because of this they were so sorrowful at the thought of His death. They would be deprived of that presence. He would no longer be with them.

How, under these circumstances, did the Lord Jesus comfort them? He promised that the Holy Spirit from heaven would so work in them a sense of the fullness of His life and of His personal presence that He would be even more intimately near and have more unbroken fellowship with them than they had ever experienced while He was upon earth.

This great promise is now the inheritance of every believer, although so many of them know so little about it. Jesus Christ, in His divine personality, in that eternal love that led Him to the cross, longs to have fellowship with us every moment of the day and to keep us in the enjoyment of that fellowship. This ought to be explained to every new convert: "The Lord loves you so much that He would have you near Him without a break, that you may experience His love." This is what every believer must learn who has felt his powerlessness for a life of prayer, of obedience, and of holiness. This alone will give us power as intercessors to conquer the world and to win souls out of it for our Lord.

2. The omnipotence of God.

How wonderful is God's power! We see it in creation; we see it in the wonders of redemption recorded in the Old Testament. We see it in the wonderful works of Christ that the Father wrought in Him, and above all in His resurrection from the dead. We are called on to believe in the Son, just as we believe in the Father. Yes, the Lord Jesus, who in His love is so unspeakably near us, is the Almighty One with whom nothing is impossible. Whatever may be in our hearts or flesh that will not submit to us, He can and will conquer. Everything that is promised in God's Word, all that is our inheritance as children of the new covenant, the Almighty Jesus can bestow upon us.

If I bow before Him in my inner chamber, then I am in contact with the eternal, unchanging power of God. If I commit myself for the day to the Lord Jesus, then I may rest assured that it is His eternal almighty power that has taken me under its protection and that will accomplish everything for me.

Oh, if we would only take time for the inner chamber so that we might experience in full reality the presence of this Almighty Jesus! What a blessedness would be ours through faith! An unbroken fellowship with an omnipotent and almighty Lord.

3. The holy love of God.

This means that He, with His whole heart, offers all His divine attributes for our service and is prepared to impart Himself to us. Christ is the revelation of His love. He is the Son of His love, the gift of His love, the power of His love.

This Jesus has sought on the cross to give an overwhelming proof of His love in His death and bloodshed, so as to make it impossible for us not to believe in that love. It is this Jesus who comes to meet us in the inner chamber; it is this Jesus who gives the positive assurance that unbroken fellowship with Him is our inheritance and will, through Him, become our experience. The holy love of God that sacrificed everything to conquer sin and bring it to nothing, comes to us in Christ to save us from every sin.

Beloved, take time to think over that word of our Lord: *"Ye believe in God, believe also in me"* (John 14:1). *"Believe me that I am in the Father.... And ye in me, and I in you"* (vv. 11, 20). That is the secret of the life of prayer. Take time in the inner chamber to bow down and worship, and wait on Him until He unveils Himself and takes possession of you and goes out with you to show how a man may live and walk in abiding fellowship with an unseen Lord.

Do you long to know how you may always experience deliverance from the sin of prayerlessness? Here you have the secret. Believe in the Son of God, and give Him time in the inner chamber to reveal Himself in His ever present nearness, as the Eternal and Almighty One, the Eternal Love who watches over you. You will experience what, up until now, you have perhaps not known—that it has not entered into the heart of man what God can do for those who love Him (1 Corinthians 2:9).

chapter 4

The Blessing of Victory

If now we are delivered from the sin of prayer-lessness and understand how this deliverance may continue to be experienced, what will be the fruit of our liberty? He who sees this correctly will, with renewed earnestness and perseverance, seek after this liberty. His life and experience will indeed be an evidence that he has obtained something of unspeakable worth. He will be a living witness of the blessing which victory has brought. Consider the following.

1. The blessedness of unbroken fellowship with God.

Think of the confidence in the Father that will take the place of the reproach and self-condemnation that was the earlier characteristic of our lives. Think of the deep consciousness that God's almighty grace has effected something in us, to prove that we really bear His image and are fitted for a life of communion with Him and are prepared to glorify Him. Think how we, notwithstanding our conviction of our nothingness, may live as true children of a King, in communion with their Father, and may manifest something of the character of our Lord Jesus in the holy fellowship with His Father that He had when on earth. Think how in the inner chamber the hour of prayer may become the happiest time in the whole day for us, and how God may use us to take a share in the carrying out of His plans, and make us fountains of blessing for the world around us.

2. The power that we may have for the work to which we are called.

The preacher will learn to receive his message directly from God, through the power of the Holy Spirit, and to deliver it in that power to the congregation. He will know where he can be filled with the love and zeal that will enable him, in his rounds of pastoral visiting, to meet and help each individual in a spirit of tender compassion. He will be able to say with Paul, *"I can do all things through Christ which strengtheneth me"* (Philippians 4:13). *"We are more than conquerors through him that loved us"* (Romans 8:37). *"We are ambassadors for Christ...we pray you in Christ's stead, be ye reconciled to God"* (2 Corinthians 5:20). These are no vain dreams or pictures of a foolish imagination. God has given us Paul as an illustration, so that, however we may differ from him in gifts or calling, yet in inner experience we may know the all-sufficiency of grace that can do all things for us as it did for him.

3. The prospect that opens before us for the future—to be consecrated to take part as intercessors in the great work of bearing on our hearts the need of the entire church and world.

Paul sought to encourage men to pray for all saints, and he tells us what a conflict he had for those who had not yet seen his face. In his personal presence he was subject to conditions of time and place, but in the Spirit he had power in the name of Christ to pray for blessing on those who had not yet heard of the Savior. In addition to his life in connection with men here on earth, far or near, he lived another, a heavenly life—one of love and of a wonderful power in prayer which he continually exercised. We can hardly form a conception of the power God will bestow, if only we get freed from the sin of prayerlessness and pray with the daring that reaches heaven and brings down blessing in the almighty name of Christ.

What a prospect! Minister and missionaries brought by God's grace to pray, let us say twice as much as formerly, with twofold faith and joy! What a difference it would make in the preaching, in the prayer meeting, in the fellowship with others! What a gentle power would come down in an inner chamber, sanctified by communion with God and

His love in Christ! What an influence would be exercised on believers, in urging them forward to the work of intercession! How greatly this influence would be felt in the church and among the heathen! What power might be exercised over ministers of other churches, and who knows how God might use us for His church throughout the whole world! Is it not worthwhile to sacrifice everything, and to beseech God without ceasing to give us real and full victory over the prayerlessness that has covered us with such shame?

Why do I now write these things and extol so highly the blessedness of victory over *the sin which doth so easily beset us*" (Hebrews 12:1) and that has so terribly robbed us of the power that God has intended for us? I can give an answer. I know all too well what low thoughts we have concerning the promises and the power of God and how prone we are always to backslide, to limit God's power, and to deem it impossible for Him to do greater things than we have seen. It is a glorious thing to get to know God in a new way in the inner chamber. That, however, is but the beginning. It is something still greater and more glorious to know God as the All-sufficient One and to wait on His Spirit to open our hearts and minds wide to receive the great things, the new things that He really longs to bestow on those who wait for Him.

God's object is to encourage faith and to make His children and servants see that they must take the trouble to understand and rely upon the unspeakable greatness and omnipotence of God, so that they may take literally and in a childlike spirit this word: *"Unto him that is able to do exceeding abundantly above all that we ask or think...be glory...throughout all ages"* (Ephesians 3:20–21). Oh, that we knew what a great and glorious God we have!

Someone may ask: "Couldn't this note of certain victory become a snare and lead to levity and pride?" Undoubtedly. What is the highest and best on earth is always liable to abuse. How, then, can we be saved from this? Through nothing so surely as through true prayer, which brings us into real contact with God. The holiness of God, sought for in persistent prayer, will cover our sinfulness. The omnipotence and greatness of God will make us feel our nothingness. Fellowship with God in Jesus Christ will lead us to the experience that there is no good thing in us, and that we can have fellowship with God only as our faith becomes a humbling of ourselves as Christ humbled Himself and we truly live in Him as He is in the Father.

Prayer is not merely coming to God to ask something from Him. It is, above all, fellowship with God and being brought under the power of His holiness and love, until He takes possession of us and stamps our entire nature with the lowliness of Christ, which is the secret of all true worship.

Yes, it is in Christ Jesus that we draw near to the Father as those who have died with Christ and are entirely done with their own lives, as those in whom He lives and whom He enables to say, *"Christ liveth in me"* (Galatians 2:20). What we have said about the work that the Lord Jesus does in us to deliver us from prayerlessness is true not only of the beginning of the life of prayer, and of the joy which a new experience of power to pray brings us; it is true for the whole life of prayer all the day long. *"Through him"* we have access to the Father (Ephesians 2:18). In this always, as in the whole spiritual life, *"Christ is all"* (Colossians 3:11). *"They saw no man, save Jesus only"* (Matthew 17:8).

May God strengthen us to a belief that there is certain victory prepared for us and that the blessing will be what the heart of man has not conceived! God will do this for those who love Him.

This does not come to us all at once. God has great patience with His children. He bears with us in our slow progress with Fatherly patience. Let each child of God rejoice in all that God's Word promises. The stronger our faith, the more earnestly will we persevere to the end.

THE MORE ABUNDANT LIFE

Our Lord spoke this word concerning the more abundant life when He said that He had come to give His life for His sheep: *"I am come that they might have life, and that they might have it more abundantly"* (John 10:10). A man may have life, and yet, through lack of nourishment, or through illness, there may be no abundance of life or power. This was the distinction between the Old Testament and the New. In the former there was indeed life, under the law, but not the abundance of grace of the New Testament. Christ had given life to His disciples, but they could receive the abundant life only through His resurrection and the gift of the Holy Spirit.

All true Christians have received life from Christ. The greater portion of them, however, know nothing about the more abundant life that He is willing to bestow. Paul speaks constantly of this. He said about himself that the grace of God was *"exceeding abundant"* (1 Timothy 1:14). *"I can do all things through Christ which strengtheneth me"* (Philippians 4:13). *"Thanks be unto God, which always causeth us to triumph in Christ"* (2 Corinthians 2:14). *"We are more than conquerors through him that loved us"* (Romans 8:37).

We have spoken of the sin of prayerlessness and the means of deliverance and how to be kept free from this sin. What has been said in these points is all included in that expression of Christ: *"I am come that they might have life, and that they might have it more abundantly."* It is of the utmost importance in order for us to understand this more abundant life, that we clearly see that for a true life of prayer nothing less is necessary than walking in an ever increasing experience of that overflow life.

It is possible for us to begin this conflict against prayerlessness depending on Christ, and looking to Him to be assisted and kept in it, and yet to be disappointed. This is the case when prayer-lessness is looked upon as the one sin against which we must strive. It must be recognized as part of the whole life of the flesh and as closely connected with other sins that spring from the same source. We forget that the entire flesh with all its affections, whether manifested in the body or soul, must be regarded as crucified and be handed over to death. We must not be satisfied with a feeble life, but must seek for an abundant life. We must surrender ourselves entirely, that the Spirit may take full possession of us. We must manifest that abundant life so completely that there may come an entire transformation in our spiritual being, by which the complete mastery of Christ and the Spirit is recognized.

What is it, then, that especially constitutes this abundant life? We cannot too often repeat it: the abundant life is nothing less than the full Jesus having the full mastery over our entire beings, through the power of the Holy Spirit. As the Spirit makes known in us the fullness of Christ, and the abundant life that He gives, it will be chiefly in three aspects.

1. As the Crucified One.

Not merely as the One who died for us, to atone for our sins, but as He who has taken us up with Himself on the cross to die with Him, and who now works out in us the power of His cross and death. You have the true fellowship with Christ when you can say, "*I am crucified with Christ*" (Galatians 2:20); He, the Crucified One, lives in me." The feelings and the disposition that were in Him, His lowliness and obedience even to the death of the cross—these were what He referred to when He said of the Holy Spirit, *"He shall take of mine, and shall show it unto you"* (John 16:15)—not as an instruction, but as childlike participation of the same life that was in Him.

Do you desire that the Holy Spirit should take full possession of you, so as to cause the crucified Christ to dwell in you? Understand then that this is just the end for which He has been given, and this He will surely accomplish in all who yield themselves to Him.

2. As the Risen One.

The Scripture frequently mentions the resurrection in connection with the wonder-working power of God, by which Christ was raised from the dead, and from which comes the assurance of *"the exceeding greatness of his power to us-ward who believe, according to the working of his mighty power, which he wrought in Christ, when he raised him from the dead"* (Ephesians 1:19–20). Do not pass hastily over these words. Turn back and read them once more, and learn the great lesson that, however powerless and weak you feel, the omnipotence of God is working in you; and, if you only believe, He will give you in daily life a share in the resurrection of His Son.

Yes, the Holy Spirit can fill you with the joy and victory of the resurrection of Christ, as the power of your daily life, here in the midst of the trials and temptations of this world. Let the Cross humble you to death. God will work out the heavenly life in you through His Spirit. Ah, how little have we understood that it is entirely the work of the Holy Spirit to make us partakers of the crucified and risen Christ, and to conform us to His life and death!

3. As the Glorified One.

The glorified Christ is He who baptizes with the Holy Spirit. When the Lord Jesus Himself was baptized with the Spirit, it was because He had humbled Himself and offered Himself to take part in John's baptism of repentance—a baptism for sinners—in Jordan. Even so, when He took upon Himself the work of redemption, He received the Holy Spirit to fit Him for His work from that hour until on the cross He *"offered himself without spot to God"* (Hebrews 9:14). Do you desire that this glorified Christ should baptize you with the Holy Spirit? Offer yourself then to Him for His service, to further His great work of making known to sinners the love of the Father.

May God help us to understand what a great thing it is to receive the Holy Spirit with power from the glorified Jesus! It means a willingness—a longing of the soul—to work for Him and, if need be, to suffer for Him. You have known and loved your Lord and have worked for Him and have had blessing in that work, but the Lord has more than that to bestow. He can so work in us, and in our brothers and sisters around us, and in the ministers of the church, by the power of the Holy Spirit, as to fill our hearts with adoring wonder.

Have you laid hold of it, my reader? The abundant life is neither more nor less than the full life of Christ as the Crucified, the Risen, the Glorified One, who baptizes with the Holy Spirit and reveals Himself in our hearts and lives as Lord of all within us.

I read not long ago an expression, "Live in what must be." Do not live in your human imagination of what is possible. Live in the Word—in the love and infinite faithfulness of the Lord Jesus. The faith that always thanks Him—not for experiences, but for the promises on which it can rely—goes on from strength to strength, still increasing in the blessed assurance that God Himself will perfect His work in us.

chapter 5

The Example of Our Lord

The connection between the prayer life and the Spirit life is close and indissoluble. It is not merely that we can receive the Spirit through prayer, but the Spirit life requires, as an indispensable thing, a continuous prayer life. I can be led continually by the Spirit only as I continually give myself to prayer.

This was very evident in the life of our Lord. A study of His life will give us a wonderful view of the power and holiness of prayer.

Consider His baptism. It was when He was baptized and prayed that heaven was opened and the Holy Spirit came down upon Him (Luke 3:21–22). God desired to crown Christ's surrender of Himself to the sinner's baptism in Jordan, which was also a surrender of Himself to the sinner's death, with the gift of the Spirit for the work that He must accomplish. But this could not have taken place had He not prayed. In the fellowship of worship, the Spirit was bestowed on Him to lead Him out into the desert to spend forty days in prayer and fasting. Turn to the first chapter of Mark:

> And at even, when the sun did set, they brought unto him all that were diseased, and them that were possessed with devils. And all the city was gathered together at the door....And in the morning, rising up a great while before day, he went out, and departed into a solitary place, and there prayed. (Mark 1:32–33, 35)

The work of the day and evening had exhausted Him. In His healing of the sick and casting out devils, power had gone out of Him. While others still slept, He went away to pray and to renew His strength in communion with His Father. He had need of this; otherwise He would not have been ready for the new day. The holy work of delivering souls demands constant renewal through fellowship with God.

Think again of the calling of the apostles as given in Luke:

> And it came to pass in those days, that he went out into a mountain to pray, and continued all night in prayer to God. And when it was day, he called unto him his disciples: and of them he chose twelve, whom also he named apostles. (Luke 6:12–13)

Is it not clear that if anyone wishes to do God's work, he must take time for fellowship with Him, to receive His wisdom and power? The dependence and helplessness of which this is an evidence open the way and give God the opportunity of revealing His power. How great was the importance of the choosing of the apostles for Christ's own work, for the early church, and for all time! It had God's blessing and seal; the stamp of prayer was on it.

Turn to Luke's gospel:

> *And it came to pass, as he was alone praying, his disciples were with him: and he asked them, saying, Whom say the people that I am?...Peter answering said, The Christ of God.* (Luke 9:18, 20)

The Lord had intended that the Father might reveal to them who He was, and for this purpose He had chosen the twelve apostles. (See John 17:6–8.) After a night of prayer, *"he chose twelve, whom also he named apostles"* (Luke 6:13). It was one of these, Peter, who said, *"Thou art the Christ, the Son of the living God"* (Matthew 16:16); and the Lord then said, *"Flesh and blood hath not revealed it unto thee, but my Father which is in heaven"* (v. 17). This great confession was the fruit of prayer.

Read further:

> *He took Peter and John and James, and went up into a mountain to pray. And as he prayed, the fashion of his countenance was altered....And there came a voice out*

> *of the cloud, saying, This is my beloved*
> *Son: hear him.*   (Luke 9:28–29, 35)

Christ had desired that, for the strengthening of
their faith, God might give them an assurance from
heaven that He was the Son of God. Prayer obtained for our Lord Jesus Himself, as well as for
His disciples, what happened on the Mount of
Transfiguration.

Does it not become still clearer that what God
wills to accomplish on earth needs prayer as its indispensable condition? And there is but one way for
Christ and believers. A heart and mouth open toward heaven in believing prayer will certainly not
be put to shame.

Read Luke 11:1:

> *As he was praying in a certain place,*
> *when he ceased, one of his disciples said*
> *unto him, Lord, teach us to pray.*

And then He gave them that inexhaustible prayer:
"Our Father which art in heaven" (v. 2). In this He
showed what was going on in His heart, when He
prayed that God's name might be hallowed, and
His kingdom come, and His will be done, and all of
this *"as in heaven, so in earth"* (v. 2). How will this
ever come to pass? Through prayer. This prayer
has been uttered through the ages by countless
millions, to their unspeakable comfort. But do not
forget this—it was born out of the prayer of our
Lord Jesus. He had been praying, and therefore
was able to give that glorious answer.

Read John 14:16: *"I will pray the Father, and he shall give you another Comforter."* The entire dispensation of the New Testament, with the wonderful outpouring of the Holy Spirit, is the outcome of the prayer of the Lord Jesus. In answer to the prayer of the Lord Jesus, and later of His disciples, the Holy Spirit will surely come. But it will be in answer to prayer like that of our Lord, in which He took time to be alone with God and in that prayer offered Himself wholly to God.

Read John 17, the most holy High Priestly Prayer! Here the Son prays first for Himself, that the Father will glorify Him by giving Him power for the Cross, by raising Him from the dead, by setting Him at His right hand. These great things could not take place except through prayer. Prayer had the power to obtain them.

Afterward, He prayed for His disciples, that the Father might preserve them from the Evil One, might keep them from the world, and might sanctify them. And then, further, He prayed for all those who through their word might believe on Him, that all might be one in love, even as the Father and the Son were One.

This prayer gives us a glimpse into the wonderful relationship between the Father and the Son and teaches us that all the blessings of heaven come continually through the prayer of Him who is at God's right hand and ever prays for us. But it teaches us, also, that all these blessings must in the same manner be desired and asked for by us. The whole nature and glory of God's blessings consist in this: they must be obtained in answer to prayer, by hearts entirely surrendered to Him, and hearts that believe in the power of prayer.

Now we come to the most remarkable instance of all. In Gethsemane we see that our Lord, according to His constant habit, consulted and arranged with the Father the work He had to do on earth. First He besought Him in agony and bloody sweat to let the cup pass from Him. When He understood that this could not be, then He prayed for strength to drink it, and surrendered Himself with the words: *"Thy will be done"* (Matthew 26:42). He was able to meet the enemy full of courage, and in the power of God He gave Himself over to the death of the cross. He had prayed.

Oh, why is it that God's children have so little faith in the glory of prayer as the great power for subjecting our own wills to that of God, as well as for the confident carrying out of the work of God in spite of our great weakness? If only we might learn from our Lord Jesus how impossible it is to walk with God, to obtain God's blessing or leading, or to do His work joyously and fruitfully, apart from close, unbroken fellowship with Him who is ever a living fountain of spiritual life and power!

Let every Christian think over this simple study of the prayer life of our Lord Jesus and endeavor from God's Word to learn what the life is that the Lord Jesus Christ bestows upon him and supports in him. It is nothing else than a life of daily prayer. Let each minister especially recognize how entirely vain it is to attempt to do the work of our Lord in any other way than that in which He did it. Let us, as workers, begin to believe that we are set free from the ordinary business of the world that we may, above everything, have time, in our Savior's name and with His Spirit and in oneness with Him, to ask for and obtain blessing for the world.

chapter 6

The Holy Spirit and Prayer

Is it not sad that our thoughts about the Holy
Spirit are so often coupled with grief and self-
reproach? Yet He bears the name of Comforter
and is given to lead us to find in Christ our chief
delight and joy. But there is something still more
sad: He who dwells within us to comfort us is often
grieved by us because we will not permit Him to
accomplish His work of love. What a cause of inex-
pressible pain to the Holy Spirit is all this prayerlessness in the church. It is the cause also of the
low vitality and utter impotence that are so often
found in us, because we are not prepared to permit
the Holy Spirit to lead us.

God grant that our meditation on the work of
the Holy Spirit may be a matter for rejoicing and
for the strengthening of our faith!

The Holy Spirit is the Spirit of prayer. He is
definitely called by this name in Zechariah 12:10:

"The spirit of grace and of supplications." Twice in Paul's Epistles there is a remarkable reference to Him in the matter of prayer. *"Ye have received the Spirit of adoption, whereby we cry, Abba, Father"* (Romans 8:15). *"God hath sent forth the Spirit of his Son into your hearts, crying, Abba, Father"* (Galatians 4:6). Have you ever meditated on these words, *"Abba, Father"*? In that name our Savior offered His greatest prayer to the Father, accompanied by the entire surrender and sacrifice of His life and love. The Holy Spirit is given for the express purpose of teaching us, from the very beginning of our Christian life onward, to utter that word in childlike trust and surrender. In one of these passages we read, "we cry"; in the other, "He cries." What a wonderful blending of the divine and human cooperation in prayer. What a proof that God—if I may say so—has done His utmost to make prayer as natural and effectual as though it were the cry of a child to an earthly father, as he says, *"Abba, Father."*

Is it not proof that the Holy Spirit is to a great extent a stranger in the church, when prayer, for which God has made such provisions, is regarded as a task and a burden? And does this not teach us to seek for the deep root of prayerlessness in our ignorance of, and disobedience to, the divine Instructor whom the Father has commissioned to teach us to pray?

If we desire to understand this truth more clearly, we must notice what is written in Romans:

> *Likewise the Spirit also helpeth our in-firmities: for we know not what we should pray for as we ought: but the Spirit itself maketh intercession for us with groanings which cannot be uttered. And he that searcheth the hearts knoweth what is the mind of the Spirit, because he maketh in-tercession for the saints according to the will of God.* (Romans 8:26–27)

Is it not clear from this that the Christian, if left to himself, does not know how to pray? God has stooped to meet us in this helplessness of ours by giving us the Holy Spirit Himself to pray for us. His operation is deeper than our thoughts or feelings and is noticed and answered by God.

Our first work, therefore, ought to be to come into God's presence, not with our ignorant prayers, not with many words and thoughts, but in the confidence that the divine work of the Holy Spirit is being carried on within us. This confidence will encourage reverence and quietness and will also enable us, in dependence on the help that the Spirit gives, to lay our desires and heart needs before God.

The great lesson for every prayer is to see to it, first of all, that you commit yourself to the leading of the Holy Spirit and, with entire dependence on Him, give Him the first place. For through Him your prayers will have a value you cannot imagine, and through Him also you will learn to speak out your desires in the name of Christ.

What a protection this faith would be against deadness and despondency in the inner chamber! Only think of it! In every prayer the Triune God takes a part: the Father who hears, the Son in whose name we pray, the Spirit who prays for us and in us. How important it is that we should be in right relationship to the Holy Spirit and understand His work!

The following points demand serious consideration.

1. Let us firmly believe, as a divine reality, that the Spirit of God's Son, the Holy Spirit, is in us.

Do not imagine that you know this and have no need to consider it. It is a thought so great and divine that it can gain an entrance to our hearts and be retained there only by the Holy Spirit Himself. *"The Spirit itself beareth witness with our spirit"* (Romans 8:16).

Our position ought to be that of reckoning with full assurance of faith that our heart is His temple, yes, that He dwells within us and rules soul and body. Let us thank God heartily as often as we pray that we have His Spirit in us to teach us to pray. Thanksgiving will draw our hearts out to God and keep us engaged with Him; it will take our attention from ourselves and give the Spirit room in our hearts.

Oh, it is no wonder that we have been prayerless and have felt this work too heavy for us, if we have sought to hold fellowship with the Eternal

God apart from His Spirit, who reveals the Father and the Son.

2. In the practice of this faith, in the certainty that the Spirit dwells and works in us, there must also be the understanding of all that He desires to accomplish in us.

His work in prayer is closely connected with His other work. We have seen in an earlier chapter that His first and greatest work is to reveal Christ in His omnipresent love and power. So the Holy Spirit will in prayer constantly remind us of Christ, of His blood and name, as the sure ground of our being heard.

He will, further, as *"the spirit of holiness"* (Romans 1:4), teach us to recognize, and hate, and be done with sin. He is the Spirit of light and wisdom (Ephesians 1:17) who leads us into the heavenly secret of God's overflowing grace. He is the Spirit of love and power (2 Timothy 1:7) who teaches us to witness for Christ and to labor for souls with tender pity.

The more closely I associate all these blessings with the Spirit, the more I will be convinced of His deity and will be ready to commit myself to His guidance, as I give myself to prayer. What a different life mine would be if I knew the Spirit as the Spirit of prayer!

3. The Spirit desires to have full possession of my life.

We pray for more of the Spirit, and we pray well, if alongside this prayer we set the truth that the Spirit wants more of me. The Spirit would possess me entirely. Just as my soul has my whole body for its dwelling place and service, so the Holy Spirit wants to have my body and soul as His dwelling place, entirely under His control. No one can continue long and earnestly in prayer without beginning to perceive that the Spirit is gently leading to an entirely new consecration, of which previously he knew nothing: "I seek You with my whole heart." (See Psalm 119:2.)

The Spirit will make such words more and more the motto of our lives. He will cause us to recognize that what remains in us of double-mindedness is truly sinful. He will reveal Christ as the Almighty Deliverer from all sin, who is always near to defend us. He will lead us in this way in prayer, to forget ourselves and make us willing to offer ourselves for training as intercessors, to whom God can entrust the carrying out of His plans, and who day and night cry to Him to avenge His church of her adversary.

God help us to know the Spirit and to reverence Him as the Spirit of prayer!

chapter 7

Sin versus the Holiness of God

To understand grace, to understand Christ properly, we must understand what sin is. And how otherwise can we come to this understanding than through the light of God and His Word? Come with me to the beginning of the Bible. See there man created by God, after His image, and pronounced by his Creator to be very good. Then sin entered as rebellion against God. Adam was driven out of Paradise and was brought, along with the untold millions of following generations, under curse and ruin. That was the work of sin. Here we learn its nature and power.

Come further on, and see the ark of Noah on Ararat. So terrible had godlessness become among men, God saw nothing but to destroy man from off the earth. That was the work of sin.

Come once more with me to Sinai. God wished to establish His covenant with a new nation—with the people of Israel. But because of man's sinfulness, He could do this only by appearing in darkness and lightning so terrible that Moses said, *"I exceedingly fear and quake"* (Hebrews 12:21). And before the end of the giving of the law, that awful message came: *"Cursed is every one that continueth not in all things which are written in the book of the law to do them"* (Galatians 3:10). It was sin which made that necessary.

Come once more with me, and this time to Calvary. There see what sin is, and the hatred and enmity with which the world cast out and crucified the Son of God. There sin reached its climax. There Christ was, by God Himself, made sin and became a curse, as the only way to destroy sin. In the agony in which He prayed in Gethsemane, that He might not drink the terrible cup, and in the agony in which on the cross, in the deep darkness of desertion, He cried out, *"My God, my God, why hast thou forsaken me?"* (Matthew 27:46), we obtain at least some faint idea of the curse and indescribable suffering which sin brings. If anything can make us hate and detest sin, it is Christ on the cross.

Come once again with me to the judgment seat of the Great Day, and see the bottomless pit of darkness wherein countless souls will be plunged under the sentence, *"Depart from me, ye cursed, into everlasting fire"* (Matthew 25:41). Oh, will not these words soften our hearts and fill us with a never-to-be-forgotten horror of sin, so that we may hate it with a perfect hatred?

And now is there anything else that can help us to understand what sin is? Yes, there is. Turn your eyes inward, and behold your own heart, and see sin there. Remember that all you have already seen of the hatefulness and godlessness of sin should teach you what sin in your own heart means; all the enmity against God, all the ruin of men, all of its inner nature of hatefulness, lie hidden in the sin you have committed. And when you acknowledge that you are a child of God and yet commit sin, allowing it sometimes to fulfill its lusts, is it not fitting that you should cry out with shame: "Woe is me, because of my sin"? *Depart from me; for I am a sinful man, O Lord"* (Luke 5:8).

One great power of sin is that it blinds men so that they do not recognize its true character. Even the Christian himself finds an excuse in the thought that he can never be perfect and that daily sin is a necessity. He is so accustomed to the thought of sinning that he has almost lost the power and ability of mourning over sin. And yet there can be no real progress in grace apart from an increased consciousness of the sin and guilt of every transgression against God. And there cannot be a more important question than this: "How can I regain the lost tenderness of conscience and become prepared really to offer to God the sacrifice of a broken heart?"

Scripture teaches us the way. Let the Christian remember what God thinks about sin—the hatred with which His holiness burns against it, the solemn sacrifice that He made to conquer sin and deliver us from it. Let him tarry in God's presence until His holiness shines upon him, and he cries out with Isaiah: *"Woe is me! for I am undone"* (Isaiah 6:5).

Let him remember the cross, and what the love of Christ had to endure there, through the unspeakable pain that sin caused Him. And let him ask if this will not teach him to hearken to the voice which says, *"Oh, do not this abominable thing that I hate"* (Jeremiah 44:4). Let him take time, so that the blood and love of the cross may exercise their full influence on him, and let him think of sin as nothing less than giving his hand to Satan and to his power. Is this not a terrible result of our prayerlessness and of our short and hasty tarrying before God that the true knowledge of sin is almost lost?

Let the believer think not only of what redemption has cost Christ, but also of the fact that Christ is offered to him, by the Holy Spirit, as a gift of inconceivable grace, through whom divine forgiveness and purification and renewing have taken possession of him. Then let him ask himself with what return such love should be repaid. If only time were taken to tarry in God's presence and ask such questions, the Spirit of God would accomplish His work of conviction of sin in us and would teach us to take an entirely new standpoint and would give us a new view of sin. The thought would begin to arise in our hearts that we have truly been redeemed, so that in the power of Christ we may live every day as partners in the great victory that Christ obtained over sin on the cross and manifest it in our walk.

What do you think? Do you begin to see that the sin of prayerlessness has had a more terrible effect than you thought at first? It is because of the hasty, superficial conversation with God that the sense of sin is so weak and that no motives have power to help you to hate and flee from sin as you should. Nothing except the hidden, humble, constant fellowship with God can teach you, as a child of God, to hate sin as God wants you to hate it. Nothing but the constant nearness and unceasing power of the living Christ can make it possible for you to rightly understand what sin is and to detest it. And without this deeper understanding of sin, there will be no thought of appropriating the victory that is made possible for you in Christ Jesus and will be wrought in you by the Spirit.

O my God, cause me to know my sin and teach me to tarry before You and to wait on You until Your Spirit causes something of Your holiness to rest upon me! O my God, cause me to know my sin, and let this drive me to listen to the promise, *"Whosoever abideth in him sinneth not"* (1 John 3:6), and to expect the fulfillment from You!

THE HOLINESS OF GOD

It has often been said that the conception of sin and of the holiness of God has been lost in the church. In the inner chamber we have the place where we may learn again how to give God's holiness the position it should have in our faith and life. If you do not know how to spend half an hour in prayer, take up the subject of God's holiness. Bow before Him. Give yourself time, and give God also time, that He and you may come into touch with one another. It is a great work but one overflowing with great blessing.

If you wish to strengthen yourself in the practice of this Holy Presence, take up the Holy Word. Take, for instance, the book of Leviticus, and notice how God gives the command seven times in various forms: "Ye shall be holy; for I am holy." (See Leviticus 11:44, 45; 19:2; 20:7, 26; 21:8; 22:32.) Still more frequent is the expression, *"I am the LORD that doth sanctify you"* (Exodus 31:13). This great thought is taken over into the New Testament. Peter said, *"Be ye holy in all manner of conversation; because it is written, Be ye holy; for I am holy"* (1 Peter 1:15–16). Paul wrote in his epistle, *"To the end he may stablish your hearts unblameable in holiness....God hath...called us...unto holiness....Faithful is he that calleth you, who also will do it"* (1 Thessalonians 3:13, 4:7, 5:24).

Nothing but the knowledge of God, as the Holy One, will make us holy. And how are we to obtain that knowledge of God, except in the inner chamber, our private place of prayer? It is a thing utterly impossible unless we take time and allow the holiness of God to shine on us. How can any man on earth obtain intimate knowledge of another man of remarkable wisdom, if he does not associate with him and place himself under his influence? And how can God Himself sanctify us, if we do not take time to be brought under the power of the glory of His holiness? Nowhere can we get to know the holiness of God, and come under its influence and power, except in the inner chamber. It has been well said: "No man can expect to make progress in holiness who is not often and long alone with God."

And what now is this holiness of God? It is the highest and most glorious and most all-embracing of all the attributes of God. *Holiness* is the most profound word in the Bible. It is a word that is at home in heaven. Both the Old and New Testaments tell us this. Isaiah heard the seraphs with veiled faces cry out, *"Holy, holy, holy, is the LORD of hosts"* (Isaiah 6:3). John heard the four living creatures say, *"Holy, holy, holy, Lord God Almighty"* (Revelation 4:8). This is the highest expression of God's glory in heaven by beings who live in His immediate presence and bow low before Him.

Dare we imagine that we, by thinking and reading and hearing, can understand or become partakers of the holiness of God? What folly! Oh, that we might begin to thank God that we have a place in the inner chamber, a place where we can be alone with Him, and take time for the prayer: "Let Your holiness, O Lord, shine more and more into our hearts, that they may become holy."

And let our hearts be deeply ashamed of our prayerlessness, through which we have made it impossible for God to impart His holiness to us. Let us beseech God fervently to forgive us for this sin and to allure us by His heavenly grace and to strengthen us to have fellowship with Him, the holy God.

I have said that the meaning of the words, *the holiness of God,* is not easily expressed. But we may begin by saying that they imply the unspeakable aversion and hatred with which God regards sin. And if you wish to understand what that means, remember that He preferred to see His Son die, rather than that sin should reign. Think of the Son of God, who gave up His life rather than act in the least matter against the will of the Father. Still further, He had such a hatred of sin that He preferred to die rather than that men should be held in sin's power. That is something of the holiness of God, which is a pledge that He will do everything for us—for you and me—to deliver us from sin. Holiness is the fire of God that will consume sin in us and make us holy sacrifices, pure and acceptable before Him (Romans 12:1). It was for this reason that the Spirit came down as fire. He is the Spirit of God's holiness, the Spirit of sanctification in us.

Oh, think over the holiness of God, and bow in lowliness before Him, until your heart is filled with the assurance of what the Holy One will do for you. Take a week, if necessary, to read and reread the words of God on this great truth, until your heart is brought under the conviction: this is the glory of the inner chamber, to converse with God the Holy One, to bow in deep humility and shame before Him, because we have so despised Him and His love through our prayerlessness. There we will receive the assurance that He will again take us into fellowship with Himself. No one can expect to understand and receive the holiness of God who is not often and long alone with God.

Someone has said that the holiness of God is the expression of the unspeakable distance by which He in His righteousness is separated from us, and yet also of the unspeakable nearness in which He in His love longs to hold fellowship with us and dwell in us. Bow in humble reverence, as you think of the immeasurable distance between you and God. Bow in childlike confidence in the unspeakable desire of His love to be united with you in the deepest intimacy, and reckon most confidently on Him to reveal something of His holiness to the soul that thirsts after Him and waits upon Him and is quiet before Him.

Notice how the two sides of the holiness of God are united in the Cross. So terrible was the aversion and anger of God against our sin that Christ was left in the thick darkness, because God, when sin was laid upon Jesus, had to hide His face from Him. And yet so deep was the love of God toward us and so deep His desire to be united to us, that He spared not His Son but gave Him over to unutterable sufferings. This was so that He might receive us, in union with Christ, into His holiness, and press us to His heart as His beloved children. It was of this suffering that our Lord Jesus said, *"I sanctify myself, that they also might be sanctified through the truth"* (John 17:19). Thus He has become of God our sanctification, and we are holy in Him.

I beseech you, do not think little of the grace that you have a holy God who longs to make you holy. Do not think little of the voice of God that calls you to give time to Him in the stillness of the inner chamber, so that He may cause His holiness to rest on you. Let it be your business every day, in the secrecy of the inner chamber, to meet the holy God. You will be repaid for the trouble it may cost you. The reward will be sure and rich. You will learn to hate sin and to regard it as accursed and conquered. The new nature will give you a horror of sin. The living Jesus, the holy God, will, as Conqueror, be your power and strength. And you will begin to believe the great promise contained in 1 Thessalonians 5:23–24: *"The very God of peace sanctify you wholly....Faithful is he that calleth you, who also will do it."*

chapter 8

Obedience and the Victorious Life

I n opposition to sin stands obedience. *"For as by one man's disobedience many were made sinners, so by the obedience of one shall many be made righteous....Ye became the servants of righteousness"* (Romans 5:19, 6:18). In connection with all that has been said about sin and the new life and the reception of the Holy Spirit, we must always give to obedience the place assigned to it by God.

It was because Christ humbled Himself and became obedient unto death, yes, the death of the cross, that God so highly exalted Him (Philippians 2:8–9). And Paul, in this connection, exhorts us: *"Let this mind be in you, which was also in Christ Jesus"* (v. 5). We see, above everything else, that the obedience of Christ, which was so pleasing to God, must become really the characteristic of our nature and of our entire walk. Just as a servant knows that he must first obey his master in all things, so the surrender to an implicit and unquestionable obedience must become the essential characteristic of our lives.

How little this is understood by Christians! How many there are who allow themselves to be misled, and rest satisfied with the thought that sin is a necessity, that one must sin every day! It would be difficult to say how great the harm is which has been done by this mistake. It is one of the chief causes why the sin of disobedience is so little recognized. I have myself heard Christians, speaking about the cause of darkness and weakness, say, half laughingly, "Yes, it is just disobedience again." We try to get rid of a servant as speedily as possible who is habitually disobedient, but it is not regarded as anything extraordinary that a child of God should be disobedient every day. Disobedience is daily acknowledged, and yet there no turning away from it.

Is this not the reason why so much prayer for the power of the Holy Spirit is offered, and yet so few answers come? Do we not read that God has given His Holy Spirit to those who obey Him (Acts 5:32)? Every child of God has received the Holy Spirit. If he uses the measure of the Holy Spirit that he has, with the definite purpose of being obedient to the utmost, then God can and will favor him with further manifestations of the Spirit's power. But if he permits disobedience to get the upper hand, day by day, he need not wonder if his prayer for more of the Spirit remains unanswered.

We have already said that we must not forget that the Spirit desires to possess more of us. How can we wholly surrender ourselves to Him other than by being obedient? The Scripture says that we must be led by the Spirit, that we must walk by the Spirit. My right relationship to the Holy Spirit is that I allow myself to be guided and ruled by Him. Obedience is the great factor in our whole relationship to God. *"Obey my voice, and I will be your God"* (Jeremiah 7:23).

Mark how the Lord Jesus, on the last night, when giving His great promise about the Holy Spirit, lays emphasis on this point. *"If ye love me, keep my commandments. And I will pray the Father, and he shall give you another Comforter"* (John 14:15–16). Obedience was essential as a preparation for the reception of the Spirit. And this thought is often repeated by Him. *"He that hath my commandments, and keepeth them, he it is that loveth me: and he that loveth me shall be loved of my Father, and I will love him, and will manifest myself to him"* (v. 21). So also in verse 23: *"If a man love me, he will keep my words: and my Father will love him, and we will come unto him, and make our abode with him."* *"If ye abide in me, and my words abide in you, ye shall ask what ye will, and it shall be done unto you"* (John 15:7). *"If ye keep my commandments, ye shall abide in my love"* (v. 10). *"Ye are my friends, if ye do whatsoever I command you"* (v. 14).

Can words more plainly or impressively declare that the whole life, following the resurrection of Christ, depends on obedience? That is the Spirit of Christ. He lived to do not His own will, but the will of the Father. And He cannot with His Spirit make an abiding home in the heart of one who does not surrender himself utterly to a life of obedience.

Alas, how few there are who are truly concerned because of this disobedience! How little it is believed that Christ really asks for and expects this from us, because He has undertaken to make it possible for us! How much is it manifested in prayer, or walk, or in the depths of the soul life, that we really endeavor to be well pleasing to the Lord in all things? We say too little in regard to our disobedience, "I will be sorry for my sin."

But is obedience really possible? It is certain for the man who believes that Christ Jesus is his sanctification and relies on Him. Just as it is possible for a man to see that Christ can at once forgive his sin, it is also possible to have faith that in Christ is a sure promise of power to accomplish all that God desires from His child. Just as through faith we found the fullness of forgiveness, so through a new act of faith we obtain a real deliverance from the dominion of the sin which has so easily beset. Then the abiding blessing of the keeping power of Christ becomes ours. This faith obtains a new insight into promises, the meaning of which was not previously understood: *"The God of peace...make you perfect in every good work to do his will, working in you that which is wellpleasing in his sight, through Jesus Christ"* (Hebrews 13:20–21). *"Unto him that is able to keep you from falling...be glory and majesty"* (Jude

24–25). *"Give diligence to make your calling and election sure: for if ye do these things, ye shall never fall"* (2 Peter 1:10). *"To the end he may stablish your hearts unblameable in holiness"* (1 Thessalonians 3:13). *"But the Lord is faithful, who shall stablish you, and keep you from evil"* (2 Thessalonians 3:3).

The soul must understand that the fulfillment of these and other promises is secured for us in Christ, and that, as certainly as the forgiveness of sin is assured to us in Him, so also is power against new or fresh attacks of sin assured to us. Then for the first time is the lesson learned accurately that faith can confidently rely upon a full Christ and His abiding protection.

This faith sheds a wholly new light on the life of obedience. Christ holds Himself responsible to work this out in me every moment, if I only trust Him for it. Then I begin to understand the important phrase with which Paul begins and closes his epistle to the Romans, "The obedience of faith." (See Romans 1:5, 16:26.)

Faith brings me to the Lord Jesus, not only to obtain the forgiveness of sin, but also that I may enjoy the power that will make it possible for me, as a child of God, to abide in Him and to be numbered among His obedient children. As His obedient children, it is written that He who has called them is holy, so they also may be holy in all manner of conversation (1 Peter 1:15). Everything depends on whether or not I believe on the whole Christ, that with the fullness of His grace He will, not now and then but every moment, be the strength of my life. Such faith will lead to an obedience which will enable me to *"walk worthy of the Lord unto all pleasing, being fruitful in every good work...strengthened with all might, according to his glorious power"* (Colossians 1:10–11).

The soul that feeds on such promises will experience, instead of the disobedience of self-effort, what the obedience of faith means. All such promises have their measure, their certainty, and their strength in the living Christ.

THE VICTORIOUS LIFE

In another chapter, we viewed the matter chiefly from the side of our Lord Jesus. We saw that there is to be found in Him—the Crucified, the Risen, and the Glorified One who baptizes with the Holy Spirit—all that is needed for a life of abundant grace. In speaking of the victorious life, we will now look at the matter from another standpoint. We want to see how a Christian can really live as a victor. We have already said that the prayer life is not something that can be improved by itself. It is so intimately bound up with the entire spiritual life that it is only when that whole life, previously marked by lack of prayer, becomes renewed and sanctified that prayer can have its rightful place of power. We must not be satisfied with less than the victorious life to which God calls His children.

You remember how our Lord, in the seven letters to the churches in the Revelation of John, concludes with a promise to those who overcome. Take the trouble of going over that seven times repeated "him that overcometh" (see Revelation 2:7, 11, 17, 26; 3:5, 12, 21) and notice what unspeakable glorious promises are given there. And they were given even to churches like Ephesus, which had lost its first love (Revelation 2:4), and Sardis, which had *"a name that thou livest,* [but] *art dead"* (Revelation 3:1); and Laodicea, with her lukewarmness and self-satisfaction (vv. 13–16). If only they would repent, they would win the crown of victory. The call comes to every Christian to strive for the crown. It is impossible to be a healthy Christian, still more impossible to be a preacher in the power of God, if everything is not sacrificed to gain the victory.

The answer to the question, as to how we attain to it, is simple. All is in Christ. *"Thanks be unto God, which always causeth us to triumph in Christ"* (2 Corinthians 2:14). *"In all these things we are more than conquerors through him that loved us"* (Romans 8:37). All depends on our right relationship to Christ, our entire surrender, perfect faith, and unbroken fellowship with Him. But you wish to know how to obtain all this. Listen once more to the simple directions as to the way by which the full enjoyment of what is prepared for you in Christ may be yours. These are a new discovery of sin, a new surrender to Christ, and a new faith in the power that will make it possible for you to persevere.

1. A new discovery of sin.

In Romans, you find described the knowledge of sin that is necessary, in repentance, for forgiveness: *"That every mouth may be stopped, and all the world may become guilty before God"* (Romans 3:19). There you took your stand, you recognized your sin more or less consciously and confessed it, and you obtained mercy. But if you would lead the victorious life, something more is needed. This comes with the experience that in you, that is, in your flesh, there *"dwelleth no good thing"* (Romans 7:18).

You have a delight in the law of God after the inner man, but you see another law in your members bringing you into captivity to the law of sin and compelling you to cry out, *"O wretched man that I am! who shall deliver me from the body of this death?"* (v. 24). It is not, as it was at conversion, when you thought over your few or many sins. This work goes much deeper. You find that, as a Christian, you have no power to do the good that you wish to do.

You must be brought to a new and deeper insight into the sin of your nature and into your utter weakness, even though you are a Christian, to live as you ought. And you will learn to cry out: "Who shall deliver me; I, wretched man, a prisoner bound under the law of sin?"

The answer to this question, is, *"I thank God through Jesus Christ our Lord"* (v. 25). Then follows the revelation of what there is in Christ. It is not just as given in Romans 3. It is more: I am in Christ

Jesus, and *"the law of the Spirit of life in Christ Jesus hath made me free from the law of sin and death"* (Romans 8:2), under which I was bound. It is the experience that the law or power of the life of the Spirit in Christ has made me free and now calls on me, in a new sense and by a new surrender, to acknowledge Christ as the bestower of the victory.

2. A new surrender to Christ.

You may have used these words *surrender* and *consecration* many times but without rightly understanding what they mean. You have been brought by the teaching of Romans 7 to a complete sense of the hopelessness of leading a true Christian life, or a true prayer life, by your own efforts. In the same way, you feel that the Lord Jesus must take you up, by His own power, in an entirely new way and must take possession of you, by His Spirit, in an entirely new measure. This alone can preserve you from constantly sinning afresh. Only this can make you really victorious. This leads you to look away from yourself, really to get free from yourself, and to expect everything from the Lord Jesus.

If we begin to understand this, we are prepared to admit that in our nature there is nothing good, that it is under a curse and is nailed with Christ to His cross. We come to see what Paul meant when he said that we are dead to sin by the death of Christ. Thus do we obtain a share of the glorious resurrection life there is in Him. By such an insight we are encouraged to believe that Christ,

through His life in us, through His continual in-
dwelling, can keep us. Just as, at our conversion,
we had no rest until we knew He had received us,
so now we feel the need of coming to Him to receive
from Him the assurance that He has really undertaken to keep us by the power of His resurrection
life. And we feel then that there must be an act as
definite as His reception of us at conversion, by
which He gives us the assurance of victory. And
although it appears to us to be too great and too
much, the man who casts himself, without plea,
into the arms of Christ will experience that He does
indeed receive us into such a fellowship as will
make us, from the beginning onward, *"more than
conquerors"* (Romans 8:37).

3. A new faith in the power that will make it possible for
you to persevere in your surrender.

Christ is prepared to take upon Himself the
care and preservation of our lives every day, and all
the day long, if we trust Him to do it. In the testimony given by many, this thought is emphasized.
They have told us that they felt themselves called
to a new surrender, to an entire consecration of life
to Christ, reaching to the smallest things, but they
were hindered by the fear of failure. The thirst after holiness, after an unbroken fellowship with Jesus, after a life of persevering childlike obedience,
drew them one way. But the question arose: "Will I
continue to be faithful?" To this question there came
no answer, until they believed that the surrender

must be made, not in their own strength, but in a power that was bestowed by a glorified Lord. He would not only keep them for the future, but He must first make possible for them the surrender of faith that expects that future grace. It was in the power of Christ Himself that they were able to present themselves to Him.

Oh, Christian, only believe that there is a victorious life! Christ, the Victor, is your Lord, who will undertake for you in everything and will enable you to do all that the Father expects from you. Be of good courage. Will you not trust Him to do this great work for you, He who has given His life for you and has forgiven your sins? Only dare, in His power, to surrender yourself to the life of those who are kept from sin by the power of God. Along with the deepest conviction that there is no good in you, confess that you see in the Lord Jesus all the goodness you need for the life of a child of God, and begin literally to live *"by the faith of the Son of God, who loved* [you], *and gave himself for* [you]" (Galatians 2:20).

Let me, for your encouragement, give the testimony of Bishop Moule, a man of deep humility and tender piety. When he first heard of Keswick,[1] he was afraid of perfectionism and would have nothing to do with it. Unexpectedly, during a vacation in Scotland, he came in contact with some friends at a small convention. There he heard an

---

[1] A town in England where a revival began with a major emphasis on God's power to keep man from sin.

address by which he was convinced how entirely
the teaching was according to Scripture. There was
no word about sinlessness in the flesh or in man. It
was a setting forth of how Jesus can keep a man
with a sinful nature from sin. The light shone into
his heart. He who had always been counted a tender Christian came into touch now with a new experience of what Christ is willing to do for one who
gives himself entirely to Him.

Listen to what he said concerning the text
from Philippians 4:13, *"I can do all things through
Christ which strengtheneth me"*:

> I dare to say that it is possible for those who
> really are willing to count on the power of the
> Lord to keep them, to lead a life in which His
> promises are taken as they stand and are found
> to be true. It is possible to cast all our care on
> Him daily and to enjoy deep peace in doing it.
> It is possible to have the thoughts and imagi-
> nations of our hearts purified in the deepest
> meaning of the word, through faith. It is possi-
> ble to see the will of God in everything and to
> receive it, not with sighing, but with singing. It
> is possible, in the inner life of desire and feel-
> ing, to lay aside all bitterness, wrath, anger,
> and evil-speaking, every day and every hour. It
> is possible, by taking complete refuge in divine
> power, to become strong through and through.
> We find that the things that formerly upset all
> our resolves to be patient or pure or humble
> furnish today an opportunity, through Him
> who loved us and works in us an agreement
> with His will and a blessed sense of His pres-
> ence and His power, to make sin powerless.

These things are divine possibilities. And because they are His work, the true experience of them will always cause us to bow lower at His feet and to learn to thirst and long for more. We cannot possibly be satisfied with anything less than—each day, each hour, each moment in Christ, through the power of the Holy Spirit—to walk with God.

Thank God, a life of victory is sure for those who have a knowledge of their inward ruin and are hopeless in themselves, but who, in the confidence of despair, have looked to Jesus. Then in faith in His power to make the act of surrender possible for them, they have done it, in His might, and now rely on Him alone every day and every hour.

chapter 9

Hints for the Inner Chamber

At the conference there was a brother who had earnestly confessed his neglect of prayer, but who was able, later, to declare that his eyes had been opened to see that the Lord really supplied grace for all that He required from us. In sincerity he asked if some hints could not be given as to the best way of spending time profitably in the inner chamber. There was no opportunity then for giving an answer. Perhaps the following thoughts may be of help.

1. As you enter the inner chamber, let your first work be to thank God for the unspeakable love that invites you to come to Him and to converse freely with Him.

If your heart is cold and dead, remember that religion is not a matter of feeling but has to do first with the will. Raise your heart to God and thank Him for the assurance you have that He looks down on you and will bless you. Through such an act of faith you honor God and draw your soul away from being occupied with itself. Think also of the glorious grace of the Lord Jesus, who is willing to teach you to pray and to give you the disposition to do so. Think, too, of the Holy Spirit who was purposely given to cry, *"Abba, Father"* (Galatians 4:6), in your heart and to help your weakness in prayer. Five minutes spent thus will strengthen your faith for your work in the inner chamber. Once more I say, begin with an act of thanksgiving and praise God for the inner chamber and the promise of blessing there.

2. You must prepare yourself for prayer by prayerful Bible study.

The great reason why the inner chamber is not attractive is that people do not know how to pray. Their stock of words is soon exhausted, and they do not know what to say further. This happens because they forget that prayer is not a soliloquy, where everything comes from one side, but it is a dialogue, where God's child listens to what the Father says, replies to it, and then asks for the things he needs.

Read a few verses from the Bible. Do not concern yourself with the difficulties contained in them. You can consider these later; but take what you understand, apply it to yourself, and ask the Father to make His Word light and power in your heart. Thus you will have material enough for prayer from the Word that the Father speaks to you; you will also have the liberty to ask for things you need. Keep on in this way, and the inner chamber will become at length, not a place where you sigh and struggle only, but one of living fellowship with the Father in heaven. Prayerful study of the Bible is indispensable for powerful prayer.

3. When you have thus received the Word into your heart, turn to prayer.

But do not attempt it hastily or thoughtlessly, as though you knew well enough how to pray. Prayer in our own strength brings no blessing. Take time to present yourself reverently and in quietness before God. Remember His greatness and holiness and love. Think over what you wish to ask from Him. Do not be satisfied with going over the same things every day. No child goes on saying the same thing day after day to his earthly father.

Conversation with the Father is colored by the needs of the day. Let your prayers be something definite, arising either out of the Word that you have read, or out of the real soul needs that you long to have satisfied. Let your prayers be so definite that you can say as you go out, "I know what I have asked from my Father, and I expect an answer."

It is a good plan sometimes to take a piece of paper and write down what you wish to pray for. You might keep such a paper for a week or more and repeat the prayers until some new need arises.

4. We are allowed to pray that we may help also in the needs of others.

What has been said is in reference your own needs. One great reason why prayer in the inner chamber does not bring more joy and blessing is that it is too selfish, and selfishness is the death of prayer.

Remember your family, your congregation, with its interests, your own neighborhood, and the church to which you belong. Let your heart be enlarged and take up the interests of missions and of the church throughout the whole world. Become an intercessor, and you will experience for the first time the blessedness of prayer, as you find out that God will make use of you to share His blessing with others through prayer. You will begin to feel that there is something worth living for, as you find that you have something to say to God, and that from heaven He will do things in answer to your prayers that otherwise would not have been done.

A child can ask his father for bread. A full-grown son converses with him about all the interests of his business and about his further purposes. A weak child of God prays only for himself, but a full-grown man in Christ understands how to consult with God over what must take place in the kingdom. Let your prayer list bear the names of those for whom you pray: your minister, and all other ministers, and the different missionary affairs with which you are connected. Thus the inner chamber will really become a wonder of God's goodness and a fountain of great joy. It will become the most blessed place on earth. It is a great thing to say, but it is the simple truth, that God will make it a Bethel, where His angels will ascend and descend, and where you will cry out, *"The LORD* [shall] *be my God"* (Genesis 28:21). He will make it also Peniel, where you will see the face of God, as a prince of God, as one who wrestled with the angel and overcame him (Genesis 32:30).

5. Do not forget the close bond between the inner chamber and the outer world.

The attitude of the inner chamber must remain with us all the day. The object of the inner chamber is to so unite us with God that we may have Him always abiding with us. Sin, thoughtlessness, and yielding to the flesh or to the world make us unfit for the inner chamber and bring a cloud over the soul. If you have stumbled or fallen, return to the inner chamber; let your first work be to invoke the blood of Jesus and to claim cleansing by it. Do not rest until by confession you have repented of and put away your sin. Let the precious blood really give you a fresh freedom of approach to God. Remember that the roots of your life in the inner chamber strike far out in body and soul so as to manifest themselves in business life. Let *"the obedience of faith"* (Romans 16:26), in which you pray in secret, rule you constantly. The inner chamber is intended to bind man to God, to supply him with power from God, to enable him to live for

God alone. Let God be thanked for the inner chamber and for the blessed life that He will enable us to experience and nourish there.

TIME

Before the creation of the world, time did not exist. God lived in eternity in a way that we little understand. With creation, time began, and everything was placed under its power. God has placed all living creatures under a law of slow growth. Think of the length of time it takes for a child to become a man in body and mind. In learning, in wisdom, in business, in handicraft, and in politics, everything somehow depends on patience and perseverance. Everything needs time.

It is just the same in religion. There can be no communion with a holy God, no fellowship between heaven and earth, no power for the salvation of the souls of others, unless much time is set apart for it. Just as it is necessary for a child, for long years, to eat and learn every day, so the life of grace depends entirely on the time men are willing to give to it day by day.

The minister is appointed by God to teach and help those who are engaged in the ordinary avocations of life to find time and to use it properly for the preservation of the spiritual life. The minister cannot do this unless he himself has a living experience of a life of prayer. His highest calling is not preaching, or speaking, or parochial visitation, but it is to cultivate the life of God daily and to be a witness of what the Lord teaches him and accomplishes in him.

Was it not so with the Lord Jesus? Why did He, who had no sin to confess, sometimes have to spend all night in prayer to God? Because the divine life had to be strengthened in communication with His Father. His experience of a life in which He took time for fellowship with God has enabled Him to share that life with us.

Oh, that each minister might understand that he has received his time from God so that he might serve Him with it! God must have the first and the best of your time for fellowship with Himself. Without this, your preaching and labor have little power. Here on earth I may spend my time for the money or the learning which I receive in exchange. The minister can exchange his time for the divine power and the spiritual blessings to be obtained from heaven. That, and nothing else, makes him a man of God and ensures that his preaching will be in the demonstration of the Spirit and power.

chapter 10

The Example of Paul

Be ye followers of me, even as I also am of Christ.
—1 Corinthians 11:1

Paul was a minister who prayed much for his congregation. Let us read his words prayerfully and calmly so that we may hear the voice of the spirit. What food for meditation!

> *Night and day praying exceedingly that we...might perfect that which is lacking in your faith....The Lord make you to increase...to the end he may stablish your hearts umblameable in holiness.*
> (1 Thessalonians 3:10, 12–13)

> *The very God of peace sanctify you wholly.*
> (1 Thessalonians 5:23)

> *Now our Lord Jesus Christ himself...comfort your hearts, and stablish*

you in every good word and work.
(2 Thessalonians 2:16–17)

Without ceasing I make mention of you always in my prayers; making request ...impart unto You some spiritual gift, to the end ye may be established.
(Romans 1:9–11)

My heart's desire and prayer to God for Israel is, that they might be saved.
(Romans 10:1)

I...cease not...making mention of you in my prayers; that...God...may give unto you the spirit of wisdom and revelation in the knowledge of him...that ye may know...what is the exceeding greatness of his power to us-ward who believe.
(Ephesians 1:15–19)

For this cause I bow my knees unto the Father...that he would grant you...to be strengthened with might by his Spirit in the inner man; that Christ may dwell in your hearts by faith; that ye, being rooted...in love...might be filled with all the fulness of God.
(Ephesians 3:14, 16–17, 19)

Always in every prayer of mine for you all making request with joy....I pray, that your love may abound yet more and more...that ye may be sincere...filled with the fruits of righteousness.
(Philippians 1:4, 9–11)

But my God shall supply all your need according to his riches in glory by Christ Jesus. (Philippians 4:19)

We...do not cease to pray for you, and to desire that ye might be filled with the knowledge of his will...that ye might walk worthy of the Lord...strengthened with all might, according to his glorious power. (Colossians 1:9–11)

I would that ye knew what great conflict I have for you...as many as have not seen my face in the flesh; that their hearts might be comforted, being knit together in love. (Colossians 2:1–2)

What a study for the inner chamber! These passages teach us that unceasing prayer formed a large part of Paul's service in the Gospel. We see the high spiritual aim that he set before himself in his work on behalf of believers, and the tender and self-sacrificing love with which he ever continued to think of the church and its needs. Let us ask God to bring each one of us, and all the ministers of His Word, to a life of which such prayer is the healthy and natural outflow. We will need to turn again and again to these pages if we would really be brought by the Spirit to the apostolic life that God has given us as an example.

Paul was a minister who asked his congregation to pray much. Read again with prayerful attention:

I beseech you, brethren, for the Lord Jesus Christ's sake, and for the love of the Spirit, that ye strive together with me in your prayers to God for me; that I may be delivered from them that do not believe in Judaea. (Romans 15:30–31)

We...trust...in God...that he will yet deliver us; ye also helping together by prayer for us. (2 Corinthians 1:9–11)

Praying always with all prayer and supplication in the Spirit, and watching thereunto with all perseverance and supplication for all saints; and for me, that utterance may be given unto me, that I may open my mouth boldly, to make known the mystery of the gospel...that therein I may speak boldly, as I ought to speak. (Ephesians 6:18–20)

For I know that this shall turn to my salvation through your prayer, and the supply of the Spirit of Jesus Christ. (Philippians 1:19)

Continue in prayer, and watch in the same with thanksgiving; withal praying also for us, that God would open unto us a door of utterance, to speak...as I ought to speak. (Colossians 4:2–4)

Finally, brethren, pray for us, that the word of the Lord may have free course, and be glorified, even as it is with you. (2 Thessalonians 3:1)

What a deep insight Paul had as to the unity of the body of Christ and the relation of the members one to another! It is as we permit the Holy Spirit to work powerfully in us that He will reveal this truth to us, and we too will have this insight. What a glimpse Paul gives us of the power of the spiritual life among these Christians, by the way in which he reckoned that at Rome and Corinth and Ephesus and Colosse and Philippi, there were men and women on whom he could rely for prayer who would reach heaven and have power with God!

Moreover, what a lesson for all ministers, to lead them to inquire if they truly appreciate the unity of the body at its right value, if they are endeavoring to train up Christians as intercessors, and if they indeed understand that Paul had that confidence because he was himself so strong in prayer for the congregation!

Let us learn the lesson and beseech God that ministers and congregations together may grow in the grace of prayer, so that their entire service and Christian life may witness that the Spirit of prayer rules them. Then we may be confident that God will avenge His own elect who cry out day and night to Him (Luke 18:7).

MINISTERS OF THE SPIRIT

What is the meaning of the expression, "The minister of the Gospel is a minister of the Spirit"? (See 2 Corinthians 3:6–8.) It means the following.

1. The preacher is entirely under the power and control of the Spirit.

Only thus may the preacher be led and used by the Spirit as He wills.

2. The Spirit must have you entirely, and always, and in all things under His power.

Many pray for the Spirit, that they may make use of Him and His power for their work. This is certainly wrong. It is He who must use you. Your relationship toward Him must be one of deep dependence and utter submission.

3. It is the Spirit in and through the preacher who will bring the Word to the heart.

There are many who think they must preach the Word only, and that the Spirit will make the Word fruitful. They do not understand that they need the Spirit. I must not be satisfied with praying to God to bless, through the operation of His Spirit, the Word that I preach. The Lord wants me to be filled with the Spirit; then I will speak properly, and my preaching will be in the manifestation of the Spirit and power.

We see this on the day of Pentecost. They were filled with the Spirit and began to speak, and spoke with power through the Spirit who was in them.

Thus we learn what the relationship of the minister toward the Spirit should be. He must have a strong belief that the Spirit is in him, that the Spirit will teach him in his daily life and will strengthen him to bear witness to the Lord Jesus in his preaching and visiting. He must live in ceaseless prayer that he may be kept and strengthened by the power of the Spirit.

When the Lord promised the apostles that they would receive power when the Holy Spirit had come upon them and commanded them to wait for Him, it was as though He had said: "Do not dare to preach without this power. It is the indispensable preparation for your work. Everything depends on it."

What then is the lesson we may learn from the phrase "ministers of the Spirit"? Alas, how little we have understood this! How little we have lived in it! How little we have experienced the power of the Holy Spirit! What must we do then? There must be deep confession of guilt that we have so constantly grieved the Spirit because we have not lived daily as His ministers. And there must be simple childlike surrender to His leading in sure confidence that the Lord will work a change in us. Finally, we must have daily fellowship with the Lord Jesus in ceaseless prayer. He will bestow on us the Holy Spirit as *"rivers of living water"* (John 7:38).

chapter 11

The Word and Prayer

Little of the Word with little prayer is death to the spiritual life. Much of the Word with little prayer gives a sickly life. Much prayer with little of the Word gives more life, but without steadfastness. A full measure of the Word and prayer each day gives a healthy and powerful life. Think of the Lord Jesus: in His youth and manhood He treasured the Word in His heart. In the temptation in the wilderness, and on every opportunity that presented itself—until He cried out on the cross in death, *"My God, my God, why hast thou forsaken me?"* (Matthew 27:46)—He showed that the Word of God filled His heart. And in His prayer life He manifested two things: first, that the Word supplies us with material for prayer and encourages us in expecting everything from God. The second is that it is only by prayer that we can live such a life that every word of God can be fulfilled in us.

How can we come to the place where the Word and prayer may each have its undivided right over us? There is only one answer. Our lives must be wholly transformed. We must get a new, a healthy, a heavenly life in which the hunger after God's Word and the thirst after God express themselves in prayer as naturally as do the needs of our earthly life. Every manifestation of the power of the flesh in us and the weakness of our spiritual life must drive us to the conviction that God will, through the powerful operation of His Holy Spirit, work out a new and strong life in us.

Oh, that we but understood that the Holy Spirit is essentially the Spirit of the Word and the Spirit of prayer! He will cause the Word to become a joy and a light in our souls, and He will also most surely help us in prayer to know the mind and will of God, and find in it our delight. If ministers wish to explain these things and to train God's people for the inheritance that is prepared for them, then they must commit ourselves from this moment forward to the leading of the Holy Spirit. They must, by faith in what He will do in them, appropriate the heavenly life of Christ as He lived it here on earth. They must have the certain expectation that the Spirit, who filled Jesus with the Word and prayer, will also accomplish that work in them.

Yes, let us believe that the Spirit who is in us is the Spirit of the Lord Jesus and that He is in us to make us truly partakers of His life. If we firmly believe this and set our hearts upon it, then there will come a change in our use of the Word and prayer such as we could not have thought possible. Believe it firmly; expect it surely.

Perhaps you are familiar with the vision of the valley of dry bones. The Lord said to the prophet, *"Prophesy upon these bones....Behold, I will cause breath to enter into you, and ye shall live"* (Ezekiel 37:4–5). When he had done this, there was a noise, and bone came together to its bone, and flesh came up, and skin covered them—but there was no breath in them. The prophesying to the bones—the preaching of the Word of God—had a powerful influence. It was the beginning of the great miracle which was about to happen, and there lay an entire army of men newly made. It was the beginning of the work of life in them, but there was no spirit there.

Then the Lord said to the prophet, *"Propehsy unto the wind...Thus saith the Lord GOD; Come from the four winds, O breath, and breathe upon these slain, that they may live"* (v. 9). And when the prophet had done this, the Spirit came upon them, and they lived and stood on their feet, a very great army. Prophesying to the bones, that is, preaching, had accomplished a great work. There lay the beautiful new bodies. But the prophesying to the Spirit, "Come, O Spirit," that is, prayer, accomplished a far more wonderful thing. The power of the Spirit was revealed through prayer.

Is not the work of our ministers mostly this prophesying to dry bones in making known the promises of God? This is followed sometimes by great results. Everything that belongs to the form of godliness has been brought to perfection; a careless congregation becomes regular and devout. But, "There is no life in them," remains true for the most part. Preaching must be followed by prayer. The preacher must come to see that his preaching is comparatively powerless to bring in a new life until he begins to take time for prayer and, according to the teaching of God's Word, strives and labors and continues in prayer, and takes no rest, and gives God no rest, until He bestows the Spirit in overflowing power.

Do you not feel that a change must come in our work? We must learn from Peter to continue in prayer, in our ministry of the Word. Just as we are zealous preachers, we must be zealous in prayer. We must, with all our power, pray unceasingly like Paul. For the prayer: *"Come...breathe on these slain,"* the answer is sure.

WHOLEHEARTEDNESS

Experience teaches us that if anyone is engaged in a work in which he is not wholehearted, he will seldom succeed. Just think of a student, or his teacher, a man of business, or a soldier. He who does not give himself wholeheartedly to his calling is not likely to succeed. And that is still more true of religion, and above all, of the high and holy task of communion in prayer with a holy God and of being always well pleasing to Him. It is because of this that God has said so impressively, *"Ye shall seek me, and find me, when ye shall search for me with all your heart"* (Jeremiah 29:13).

Many of God's servants has said, "I seek You with my whole heart." Have you ever thought how many Christians there are of whom it is all too plain that they do not seek God wholeheartedly? When they were in trouble over their sins, they seemed to seek God with their whole hearts, but then they discovered they had been pardoned. One could see by their lives that they were religious, but no one would think, "This man has surrendered himself with his whole heart to follow God and to serve Him as the supreme work of his life."

How is it with you? What does your heart say? While you, as a minister for instance, have given yourself up with wholehearted devotion to fulfill your office faithfully and zealously, will you not perhaps acknowledge, "I fear, or rather I am convinced, that my unsatisfactory prayer life is to be attributed to nothing else than that I have not lived with a wholehearted surrender of all on earth that could hinder me in fellowship with God." What a deeply important question to consider in the inner chamber and to give the answer to God! How important to arrive at a plain answer and to utter it all before God! Prayerlessness cannot be overcome as an isolated thing. It is in the closest relationship to the state of the heart. True prayer depends on an undivided heart.

You may say, "But I cannot give myself that undivided heart that enables me to say, 'I seek God with my whole heart.'" No, that is impossible for you, but God will do it. "I will give them hearts to fear me." (See Jeremiah 32:40.) "I will write my law (as a power of life) in their hearts." (See Jeremiah 31:33.) Such promises serve to awaken desire. However weak the desire may be, if there is but the sincere determination to strive after what God holds out to us, then He will Himself work in our hearts both to will and to do. It is the great work of the Holy Spirit in us to make us willing and to enable us to seek God with the whole heart.

chapter 12

"Follow Me"

The Lord did not speak the words, *"Follow me"* (Matthew 4:19), to all who believed on Him, or who hoped to be blessed by Him, but only to those whom He would make fishers of men. He said this not only at the first calling of the apostles, but also later on to Peter, *"Henceforth thou shalt catch men"* (Luke 5:10). The holy art of winning souls, of loving and saving them, can be learned only in close and persistent communion with Christ. What a lesson for ministers and for Christian workers and others!

This communion was the great and special privilege of His disciples. The Lord chose them that they might always be with and near Him. We read of the choice of the twelve apostles in Mark 3:14: *"And he ordained twelve, that they should be with him, and that he might send them forth to preach."* So also our Lord said on the last night, *"And ye also shall bear witness, because ye have been with me from the beginning"* (John 15:27).

This fact was noticed by outsiders—thus, for instance, the woman who spoke to Peter, *"This man was also with him"* (Luke 22:56). So in the Sanhedrin, *"They took knowledge of them, that they had been with Jesus"* (Acts 4:13). The chief characteristic and indispensable qualification for the man who will bear witness to Christ is that he has been with Him. Continuous fellowship with Christ is the only school for the training of believers in the Holy Spirit. What a lesson for all Christians! It is only he who, like Caleb (see Numbers 14:24), follows the Lord fully who will have power to teach other souls the art of following Jesus. But what an unspeakable grace that the Lord Jesus Himself would train us after His own likeness, so that others may learn from us! Then we might say with Paul to our converts, *"Ye became followers of us, and of the Lord"* (1 Thessalonians 1:6) *"Be ye followers of me, even as I also am of Christ"* (1 Corinthians 11:1).

Never was there a teacher who took such trouble with his scholars as Jesus Christ will with us who preach His Word. He will spare no pains; no time will be too precious or too long for Him. In the love that brought Him to the cross, He would have intimate conversation with us, fashion us, sanctify us, and make us fit for His holy service. Dare we still complain that it is too much for us to spend so much time in prayer? Will we not commit ourselves entirely to the love which gave up all for us, and look upon it as our greatest happiness now to hold fellowship with Him daily? Oh, all you who long for blessing in your ministry, He calls you to be with Him! Let this be the greatest joy of your life; it will be the surest preparation for blessing in your service. Oh, my Lord, draw me, help me, hold me fast, and teach me how to daily live in Your fellowship by faith.

THE HOLY TRINITY

God is an ever flowing fountain of pure love and blessedness.

Christ is the reservoir wherein the fullness of God was made visible as grace, and has been opened for us.

The Holy Spirit is the stream of living water that flows from under the throne of God and of the Lamb.

The redeemed, God's believing children, are the channels through which the love of the Father, the grace of Christ, and the powerful operation of the Spirit are brought to the earth, there to be imparted to others.

What an impression we gain here of the wonderful partnership into which God takes us up as dispensers of the grace of God! Prayer, when we chiefly pray for ourselves, is but the beginning of the life of prayer. The glory of prayer is that we have power as intercessors to bring the grace of the Lord Jesus Christ, and the energizing power of the

Holy Spirit, upon those souls who are still in darkness.

The more surely the channel is connected with the reservoir, the more certainly will the water flow unhindered through it. The more we are occupied in prayer with the fullness of Christ and with the Spirit who proceeds from Him, and the more firmly we abide in fellowship with Him, the more surely will our lives be happy and strong. This, however, is still only a preparation for the reality. The more we give ourselves up to fellowship and converse with the Triune God, the sooner will we receive the courage and ability to pray down blessing on souls, on ministers, and on the church around us.

Are you truly a channel that is always open, so that the water may flow through you to the thirsty ones in the dry land? Have you offered yourself unreservedly to God, to become a bearer of the energizing operations of the Holy Spirit?

Is it not, perhaps, because you have thought only of yourself in prayer that you have experienced so little of the power of prayer? Do you understand that the new prayer life into which you have entered in the Lord Jesus can be sustained and strengthened only by the intercession in which you labor for the souls around you, to bring them to know the Lord? Oh, meditate on this—God an ever flowing fountain of love and blessing, and I, His child, a living channel through which the Spirit and life can be brought to the earth every day!

LIFE AND PRAYER

Our lives have a great influence on our prayers, just as in the same way our prayers influence our lives. The entire life of man is a continuous prayer, to nature or to the world, to provide for his wants and make him happy. This natural prayer and desire of the heart can be so strong in a man who also prays to God that the words of prayer that his mouth utters cannot be heard. At times God cannot hear the prayer of your lips because the desires of your heart after the world cry out to Him much more strongly and loudly.

Life exercises a mighty influence over prayer. A worldly life, a self-seeking life, makes prayer powerless and an answer impossible. With many Christians there is a conflict between life and prayer, and life holds the upper hand. But prayer can also exercise a mighty influence over life. If I give myself entirely to God in prayer, then prayer can conquer the life of the flesh and sin. The entire life may be brought under the control of prayer. Prayer can change and renew the whole life, because prayer calls in and receives the Lord Jesus and the Holy Spirit to purify and sanctify the life.

Many think that they must, with their defective spiritual life, work themselves up to pray more. They do not understand that only in proportion as the spiritual life is strengthened can the prayer life increase. Prayer and life are inseparably connected. What do you think? Which of these has the stronger influence over you—prayer for five or ten minutes, or the whole day spent in the desires of the world? Let it not surprise you if your prayers are not answered. The reason may easily lie here; your life and your prayers are at strife with each other; your heart is more wholly devoted to living than to prayer. Learn this great lesson: my prayer must rule my whole life. What I request from God in prayer is not decided in five or ten minutes. I must learn to say, "I have prayed with my whole heart." What I desire from God must really fill my heart the whole day; then the way is open for a certain answer.

Oh, the sacredness and power of prayer if it takes possession of the heart and life! It keeps one constantly in fellowship with God. We can then literally say, "I wait on You all the day." Let us be careful to consider not only the length of the time we spend with God in prayer, but the power with which our prayers take possession of our whole lives.

PERSEVERANCE IN PRAYER

"It is not reason," said Peter, *"that we should leave the word of God, and serve tables"* (Acts 6:2). For that work deacons were chosen. And this word of Peter serves for all time and for all who are set apart as ministers. *"We will give ourselves continually to prayer, and to the ministry of the word"* (v. 4). Dr. Alexander Whyte, in an address, once said: "I

sometimes wonder, when my salary is paid to me so punctually, and the deacons have performed their part faithfully; have I been so faithful in my part, in persevering in prayer and the ministry of the Word?" Another minister has said: "How surprised people would be if I proposed to divide my time between these two equally—one-half given to prayer, the other to the ministry of the Word!"

Notice, in the case of Peter recorded in Acts, chapter 10, what perseverance in prayer meant. He went up on the roof to pray. There, in prayer, he received heavenly instruction as to his work among the heathen. There, the message from Cornelius came to him. There, the Holy Spirit said to him, *"Arise...and go with them"* (v. 20). And from there he went to Caesarea, where the Spirit was so unexpectedly outpoured on the heathen. All this is to teach us that it is through prayer God will give the instruction of His Spirit to make us understand His will, to let us know with whom we are to speak, to give us the assurance that His Spirit will make His Word powerful through us.

Have you ever earnestly thought over why ministers have a salary and a parsonage and are set free from the need of following earthly business? It is for nothing else than that they should continue in prayer and the ministry of the Word. That will be their wisdom and power. That will be the secret of a blessed service of the Gospel.

No wonder there is complaint about the ineffective spiritual life in minister and congregation, when what is of prime importance, perseverance in prayer, does not hold its rightful first place.

Peter was able to speak and act as he did because he was filled with the Spirit. Let us not be satisfied with anything less than hearty surrender to an undivided appropriation of the Spirit, as Leader and Lord of our lives. Nothing less will help us. Then, for the first time, we will be able to say, "[God] *hath made us able ministers of...the spirit*" (2 Corinthians 3:6).

CARNAL OR SPIRITUAL?

There is a great difference between these two states that is little understood or pondered. The Christian who walks in the Spirit and has crucified the flesh is spiritual (Galatians 5:24). The Christian who walks after the flesh and wishes to please the flesh is carnal (Romans 13:14). The Galatians, who had begun in the Spirit, were ending in the flesh. Yet there were among them some spiritual members who were able to restore the wandering with meekness.

What a difference between the carnal and the spiritual Christian! (See 1 Corinthians 3:1–3.) With the carnal Christian there may be much religion and much zeal for God and for the service of God. But it is for the most part in human power. With the spiritual, on the other hand, there is a complete subjection to the leading of the Spirit, a deep sense of weakness and entire dependence on the work of

Christ; it is a life of abiding fellowship with Christ, wrought out by the Spirit.

How important it is for me to find out and plainly acknowledge before God whether I am spiritual or carnal! A minister may be very faithful in his orthodoxy, and be most zealous in his service, and yet be so chiefly in the power of human wisdom and zeal. And one of the signs of this is that there is little pleasure or perseverance in fellowship with Christ through prayer. Love of prayer is one of the marks of the Spirit.

What a change is necessary for a Christian who is chiefly carnal to become truly spiritual! At first he cannot understand what must happen, or how it can come to pass. The more the truth dawns upon him, the more he is convinced that it is impossible, unless God does it. Yet to believe truly that God will do it requires earnest prayer. Quiet retirement and meditation are indispensable, along with the death of all confidence in ourselves. But along this road there ever comes the faith that God can, God is willing, God will do it. The soul that earnestly clings to the Lord Jesus will be led by the Spirit to this faith.

How will you be able to avoid having someone say to you, *"I...could not speak unto you as unto spiritual, but as unto carnal, even as unto babes in Christ"* (1 Corinthians 3:1)? It is impossible unless you have the experience of having passed from the one state to the other. God will teach you. Persevere in prayer and faith.

chapter 13

George Müller and Hudson Taylor

Just as God gave the apostle Paul as an example in his prayer life for Christians of all time, so He has also given George Müller in these latter days as a proof to His church how literally and wonderfully He still always hears prayer. It is not only that He gave him in his lifetime over a million pounds sterling to support his orphanages, but Mr. Müller also stated that he believed that the Lord had given him more than thirty thousand souls in answer to prayer. And that not only from among the orphans, but also many others for whom he—in some cases for fifty years—had prayed faithfully every day, in the firm faith that they would be saved. When he was asked on what ground he so firmly believed this, his answer was, "There are five conditions which I always endeavor to fulfill; by observing these I have the assurance of answer to my prayer:

I have not the least doubt because I am assured that it is the Lord's will to save them, for He wills that all men should be saved and come to the knowledge of the truth (1 Timothy 2:4); and we have the assurance *"that, if we ask any thing according to his will, he heareth us"* (1 John 5:14).

I have never pleaded for their salvation in my own name, but in the blessed name of my precious Lord Jesus, and on His merits alone (John 1:14).

I always firmly believed in the willingness of God to hear my prayers (Mark 11:24).

I am not conscious of having yielded to any sin, for *"if I regard iniquity in my heart, the Lord will not hear me"* (Psalm 66:18) when I call.

I have persevered in believing prayer for more than fifty-two years for some, and will continue until the answer comes: *"Shall not God avenge his own elect, which cry day and night unto him?"* (Luke 18:7).

Take these thoughts into your hearts and practice prayer according to these rules. Let prayer be not only the utterance of your desires, but a fellowship with God, until we know by faith that our prayers are heard.

The way George Müller walked is the new and living way to the throne of grace, which is open for us all.

HUDSON TAYLOR

When Hudson Taylor, as a young man, had given himself unreservedly to the Lord, there came to him a strong conviction that God would send him to China. He had read of George Müller and how God had answered his prayers for his own support and that of his orphans, and he began to ask the Lord to teach him how to trust Him in the same way. He felt that if he would go to China with such faith, he must first begin to live by faith in England. He asked the Lord to enable him to do this. He had a position as a doctor's dispenser and asked God to help him not to ask for his salary, but to leave it to God to move the heart of the doctor to pay him at the right time. The doctor was a good-hearted man, but very irregular in payment. This cost Taylor much trouble and struggle in prayer because he believed, as did George Müller, that the word, *"Owe no man any thing"* (Romans 13:8) was to be taken literally, and that debt should not be incurred.

So he learned the great lesson to move men through God—a thought of deep meaning, which later on became an unspeakably great blessing to him in his work in China. He relied on this truth: in the conversion of the Chinese, in the awakening of Christians to give money for the support of the work, and in finding suitable missionaries who would hold to faith's rule of conduct, that we should make our desires known to God in prayer, and then rely on God to move men to do what He would have done.

After he had been in China for some years, he prayed that God would give twenty-four missionaries, two for each of the eleven provinces and Mongolia, each with millions of souls and with no missionaries. God did it. But there was no society to send them out. He had indeed learned to trust God for his own support, but he dared not take upon himself the responsibility of the twenty-four, if possibly they had not sufficient faith. This cost him severe conflict, and he became very ill under it, until at last he saw that God could as easily care for the twenty-four as for himself. He undertook it in a glad faith. And so God led him, through many severe trials of faith, to trust Him fully. These twenty-four increased, in the course of time, to a thousand missionaries who relied wholly on God for support. Other missionary societies have acknowledged how much they have learned from Hudson Taylor, as a man who stated and obeyed this law: Faith may rely on God to move men to do what His children have asked of Him in prayer.

LIGHT FROM THE INNER CHAMBER

But thou, when thou prayest, enter into thy closet, and when thou hast shut thy door, pray to thy Father which is in secret; and thy Father which seeth in secret shall reward thee openly. (Matthew 6:6)

Our Lord had spoken of the prayer of the hypocrites who desire to be seen of men and also of the prayer of the heathen who trust in the multitude of their words. They do not understand that prayer has no value unless it is addressed to a personal God who sees and hears. In Matthew 6:6, our Lord teaches us a wonderful lesson concerning the inestimable blessing which the Christian may have in his inner chamber. In order to understand the lesson properly, we must notice the light that the inner chamber sheds on the following.

1. The wonderful love of God.

Think of God, His greatness, His holiness, His unspeakable glory, and then on the inestimable privilege to which he invites His children, that each one of them, however sinful or feeble he may be, may have access to Him every hour of the day and converse with Him as long as he wishes. If he enters his inner chamber, then God is ready to meet him, to have fellowship with him, to give him the joy and strength that he needs with the living assurance in his heart that He is with him and will undertake for him in everything. In addition, He promises that He will enrich him in his outward life and work with those things that he has asked for in secret. Should we not cry out with joy? What an honor! What a salvation! What an overflowing supply for every need!

One may be in the greatest distress, or may have fallen into the deepest sin, or may in the ordinary course of life desire temporal or spiritual blessing; he may desire to pray for himself or for those belonging to him, or for his congregation or church; he may even become an intercessor for the whole world—the promise for the inner chamber covers all: *"Pray to thy Father which is in secret; and thy Father...shall reward thee openly."*

We might well suppose that there is no place on earth so attractive to the child of God as the inner chamber with the presence of God promised, where he may have unhindered communion with the Father. The happiness of a child on earth if he enjoys the love of his father, the happiness of a friend as he meets a beloved benefactor, the happiness of a subject who has free access to his king and may stay with him as long as he wishes, these are nothing compared with this heavenly promise. In the inner chamber you can converse with your God as long and as intimately as you desire; you can rely on His presence and fellowship.

Oh, the wonderful love of God in the gift of an inner chamber sanctified by such a promise! Let us thank God every day of our lives for it as the gift of His wonderful love. In this sinful world He could devise nothing more suitable for our needs than a fountain of unspeakable blessing.

2. The deep sinfulness of man.

We might have thought that every child of God would have availed himself with joy of such an invitation. But, see! What is the response? There comes a cry from all lands that prayer in the inner chamber is, as a general rule, neglected by those who call themselves believers. Many make no use of it; they go to church, they confess Christ, but they know little of personal communication with God. Many make a little use of it, but in a spirit of haste, and more as a matter of custom, or for the easing of conscience. Therefore, they cannot speak of any joy or blessing in it. And, what is sadder, many who know something of its blessedness confess that they know little about faithful, regular, and happy fellowship with the Father, all the day, as something that is as necessary as their daily bread.

What is it, then, that makes the inner chamber so powerless? Is it not the deep sinfulness of man, and the aversion of his fallen nature for God, which make the world with its fellowship more attractive than being alone with the heavenly Father? Is it not that Christians do not believe the Word of God where that Word declares that the flesh that is in them is enmity against God (Romans 8:7), and that they walk too much after the flesh, so that the Spirit cannot strengthen them for prayer? Is it not that Christians allow themselves to be deprived by Satan of the use of the weapon of prayer, so that they are powerless to overcome him? Oh, the deep sinfulness of man! We have no greater proof of it than this dishonor that is done to the unspeakable love that has given us the inner chamber.

And what is still sadder is that even ministers of Christ acknowledge that they know they pray too little. The Word tells them that their only power lies in prayer; through that only, and through that certainly, they can be clothed with power from on high for their work. But it seems as though the power of the world and the flesh have deceived them. While they devote time to, and manifest zeal in, their work, what is the most necessary of all is neglected. And there is not the desire or strength for prayer to obtain the indispensable gift of the Holy Spirit to make their work fruitful. God give us grace to understand in the light of the inner chamber the deep sinfulness of our nature.

3. The glorious grace of Christ Jesus.

Is there, then, no hope of a change? Must it always be this way? Or is there a means of recovery? Thank God, there is!

The man through whom God has made known to us the message of the inner chamber is no other than our Lord Jesus Christ, who saves us from our sins. He is able and willing to deliver us from this sin, and He will deliver. He has not undertaken to redeem us from all our other sins and leave us to deal with the sin of prayerlessness in our own strength. No, in this also we may come to Him and cry out, *"Lord, if thou wilt, thou canst make me clean"* (Matthew 8:2). *"Lord, I believe; help thou mine unbelief"* (Mark 9:24).

Do you wish to know how you may experience this deliverance? By none other than the well-known way along which every sinner must come to

Christ. Begin by acknowledging, by confessing before Him in a childlike and simple manner, the sin of neglecting and desecrating the inner chamber. Bow before Him in deep shame and sorrow. Tell Him that your heart has deceived you by the thought that you could pray as you ought. Tell Him that through the weakness of the flesh, and the power of the world, and self-confidence, you have been led astray and that you have no strength to do better. Let this be done heartily. You cannot by your resolution and effort put things right.

Come in your sin and weakness to the inner chamber, and begin to thank God, as you have never thanked Him, that the grace of the Lord Jesus will surely make it possible for you to converse with your Father as a child ought to do. Hand over afresh to the Lord Jesus all your sin and misery, as well as your whole life and will, that He may cleanse and take possession of you and rule over you as His very own.

Even though your heart is cold and dead, persevere in the exercise of faith that Christ is an almighty and faithful Savior. You may be sure that deliverance will come. Expect it, and you will begin to understand that the inner chamber is the revelation of the glorious grace of the Lord Jesus. This grace makes it possible for us to do what we could not do ourselves; that is, to have fellowship with God and to experience the desire and power of remaining in that intimate fellowship as we walk with God.

chapter 14

The Spirit of the Cross

We seek sometimes for the operation of the Spirit, with the object of obtaining more power for work, more love in life, more holiness in the heart, more light on Scripture or on our path. And yet all these gifts are only subordinate to what is the great purpose of God. The Father has bestowed the Spirit on the Son, and the Son has given Him to us, with the one great object of revealing and glorifying Christ Jesus Himself in us.

The heavenly Christ must become for us a real living personality, always with us and in us. Our life on earth must be lived every day in the unbroken and holy fellowship of our Lord Jesus in heaven. This must be the first and the greatest work of the Holy Spirit in believers, that they should know and experience Christ as the life of their lives. God desires that we should become strengthened with might by His Spirit in the inner man, that Christ may dwell in our hearts through faith, and that we may be filled with His love unto all the fullness of God (Ephesians 3:16–19).

This was the secret of the joy of the first disciples. They had received the Lord Jesus, whom they feared they had lost, as the heavenly Christ into their hearts.

And this was their preparation for Pentecost: they were entirely taken up with Him. He was literally their all. Their hearts were empty of everything, so that the Spirit might fill them with Christ. In the fullness of the Spirit they had power for a life and service such as the Lord desired. Is this, now, the great object in our desires, in our prayers, in our experience? May the Lord teach us to know that the blessing for which we have so earnestly prayed can be preserved and increased in no other way than through intimate fellowship with Christ in the inner chamber, practiced and cultivated every day.

And yet it has seemed to me that there was a still deeper secret of Pentecost to be discovered. The thought came that perhaps our conception of the Lord Jesus in heaven was limited. We think of Him in the splendor, the glory of God's throne. We also think of the unsearchable love that moved Him to give Himself for us. But we forget too often that, above all, it is as the Crucified One He was known here on earth, and that, above all, it is as the Crucified One He has His place on the throne of God. *"And, lo, in the midst of the throne...stood a Lamb as it had been slain"* (Revelation 5:6).

Yes, it is as the Crucified One that He is the object of the Father's eternal good pleasure and of the worship of the entire creation. And it is, therefore, of the first importance that we here on earth should know and have experience of Him as the Crucified One, so that we may make men see what His nature and ours is, and what the power is that can make them partakers of salvation.

The Cross is Christ's highest glory. The Holy Spirit neither has done nor can do anything greater or more glorious than He did when He empowered Jesus to go to that cross: *"Christ...through the eternal Spirit offered himself without spot to God"* (Hebrews 9:14). In the same way, the Holy Spirit can do nothing greater or more glorious for us than to take us up into the fellowship of that Cross, and to work in us the same spirit of the Cross that was seen in our Lord Jesus. In a word, the question arose whether this was not the real reason why our prayers for the powerful operation of the Holy Spirit could not be answered, because we had sought too little to receive the Spirit, in order that we might know and become like the glorified Christ in the fellowship of His Cross.

Is this not the deepest secret of Pentecost? The Spirit comes to us from the cross, where He strengthened Christ to offer Himself to God. He comes from the Father, who looked down with un- speakable good pleasure at the humiliation and obedience and self-sacrifice of Christ, as the highest proof of His surrender to Him. He comes from Christ, who through the cross was prepared to receive from the Father the fullness of the Spirit, that He might share it with the world. He comes to reveal Christ to out hearts, as the Lamb slain in the midst of the throne, so that we on earth may worship Him as they do in heaven. He comes, chiefly, to impart to us the life of the crucified Christ, so that we may be able to say truly, *"I am crucified with Christ: nevertheless I live; yet not I, but Christ liveth in me"* (Galatians 2:20).

To understand this secret in any way, we must first meditate on what the meaning and what the worth of the Cross is.

THE MIND OF THE CRUCIFIED CHRIST

The Cross must necessarily be viewed from two standpoints. The first is the work it has accomplished—the pardon and conquest of sin. This is the first message with which the Cross comes to the sinner. It proclaims to him free and full deliverance from the power of sin. And then the second is the spirit or inner nature that was manifested there. We find this expressed in Philippians 2:8: *"He humbled himself, and became obedient unto death, even the death of the cross."* Here we see self-abasement to the lowest place that could be found under the burden of our sin and curse, obedience to the uttermost to all the will of God, self-sacrifice to the death of the cross. These three words reveal to us the holy perfection of His Person and work. Therefore, God has so greatly exalted Him. It was the spirit of the Cross that made Him the object of His Father's good pleasure, of the worship of the angels, of the love and confidence of all the redeemed. The self-abasement of Christ, His obedience to the will of God even to death, His self-sacrifice even to the death of the cross—these made Him the *"Lamb, as it had been slain,"* standing *"in the midst of the throne"* (Revelation 5:6).

THE SPIRIT OF THE CROSS IN US

All that Christ was, He was for us and desires to become in us. The spirit of the Cross was His blessedness and glory. It should be this even more for us. He desires to manifest His likeness in us and to give us a full share of all that is His. Thus Paul wrote the words we have so often quoted: *"Let this mind be in you, which was also in Christ Jesus"* (Philippians 2:5). Elsewhere he wrote, *"We have the mind of Christ"* (1 Corinthians 2:16).

The fellowship of the Cross in not only a holy duty for us, but also an unspeakably blessed privilege, which the Holy Spirit Himself will make ours according to the promise: *"He shall take of mine, and shall show it unto you"* (John 16:15); *"He shall glorify me"* (v. 14). The Holy Spirit worked this disposition in Christ, and He will also work it in us.

chapter 15

Taking Up the Cross

When the Lord told His disciples that they must take up the cross and follow Him, they could have little understanding of His meaning. He wished to encourage them to earnest thought and so prepare them for the time when they would see Him carrying His cross. From the Jordan, where He had presented Himself to be baptized and reckoned among sinners, onward, He carried the Cross always in His heart. That is to say, He was always conscious that the sentence of death, because of sin, rested on Him, and that He must bear it to the uttermost. As the disciples thought on this and wondered what He meant by it, only one thing was clear to them: it was the thought of a man who was sentenced to death, and carried his cross to the appointed place.

Christ had said at the same time, *"He that loseth his life... shall find it"* (Matthew 10:39). He

taught them that they must hate their own lives.
Their natures were so sinful that nothing less than
death could meet their needs; they deserved nothing less than death.

So the conviction gradually dawned upon
them that the taking up of the cross meant, "I am
to feel that my life is under sentence of death, and
that under the consciousness of this sentence I
must constantly surrender my flesh, my sinful nature, to death." So they were slowly prepared to see
later on that the cross that Christ had carried was
the one power truly to deliver from sin, and that
they must first receive from Him the true Cross
spirit. They must learn from Him what self-
humiliation in their weakness and unworthiness
was to mean; what the obedience was that crucified
their own will in all things, in the greatest as well
as in the least; what the self-denial was that did not
seek to please the flesh or the world. *"Take up
[your] cross, and follow me"* (Matthew 16:24)—that
was the word with which Jesus prepared His disciples for the great thought that His mind and inner
nature might become theirs, that His cross might
indeed become their own.

CRUCIFIED WITH CHRIST

The lesson that the Lord wished His disciples
to learn from His statement concerning the taking
up of the cross and the losing of their life finds its
expression in the words of Paul. Naturally, he was

speaking after Christ had died on the cross and been exalted on high, and the Spirit had been poured out.

Paul said, *"I am crucified with Christ"* (Galatians 2:20); *"God forbid that I should glory, save in the cross of our Lord Jesus Christ, by whom the world is crucified unto me, and I unto the world"* (Galatians 6:14). He wished that every believer would live in a manner that proved he was crucified with Christ. He wished us to understand that the Christ who comes to dwell in our hearts is the crucified Christ who will Himself, through His life, impart to us the true mind of the Cross. He told us that *"our old man is crucified with him"* (Romans 6:6). Yes, more, *"They that are Christ's have crucified the flesh"* (Galatians 5:24).

When we have received by faith the crucified Christ, we give over the flesh to the death sentence that was executed to the full on Calvary. Paul said, *"We have been planted together in the likeness of his death"* (Romans 6:5), and that therefore we must reckon that we are *"dead indeed unto sin"* (v. 6) in Christ Jesus.

These words of the Holy Spirit, through Paul, teach us that we must abide constantly in the fellowship of the Cross, in fellowship with the crucified and living Lord Jesus. It is the soul that continuously lives under the cover, shelter, and deliverance of the cross that alone can expect to continuously glory in Christ Jesus and in His abiding nearness.

THE FELLOWSHIP OF THE CROSS

There are many who place their hope for salvation in the redemption of the Cross who understand little about the fellowship of the Cross. They rely on what the Cross has purchased for them, on forgiveness of sin and peace with God. But they can often live for a length of time without fellowship with the Lord Himself. They do not know what it means to strive every day after heart communion with the crucified Lord as He is seen in heaven: *"A Lamb...in the midst of the throne"* (Revelation 5:6). Oh, that this vision might exercise its spiritual power upon us. Then we will really experience every day that as truly as the Lamb is seen there on the throne, so we may have the power and experience of His presence here!

Is it possible? Without a doubt it is. Why did that great miracle happen, and why was the Holy Spirit given from heaven, if it were not to make the glorified Jesus, the Lamb standing, as slain, in the midst of the throne, present with us here in our earthly surroundings?

chapter 16

The Holy Spirit and the Cross

The Holy Spirit always leads us to the cross. It was so with Christ. The Spirit taught Him and enabled Him to offer Himself without spot to God (Hebrews 9:14). It was so with the disciples. The Spirit, with whom they were filled, led them to preach Christ as the Crucified One. Later on He led them to glory in the fellowship of the Cross when they were deemed worthy to suffer for Christ's sake.

And the Cross directed them again to the Spirit. When Christ had borne the cross, He received the Spirit from the Father, that the Spirit might be poured out. When the three thousand bowed before the Crucified One (Acts 2:41), they received the promise of the Holy Spirit. When the disciples rejoiced in their experience of the fellowship of the Cross, they received the Holy Spirit afresh. The union between the Spirit and the Cross is indissoluble; they belong inseparably to one another. We see this especially in the epistles of Paul.

Jesus Christ hath been evidently set forth, crucified among you....Received ye the Spirit by the works of the law, or by the hearing of faith? (Galatians 3:1–2)

Christ hath redeemed us from the curse of the law...that we might receive the promise of the Spirit through faith.
(Galatians 3:13–14)

God sent forth his Son...to redeem them that were under the law...and...hath sent forth the Spirit of his Son into your hearts. (Galatians 4:4–6)

And they that are Christ's have crucified the flesh....If we live in the Spirit, let us also walk in the Spirit. (Galatians 5:24–25)

Ye also are become dead to the law by the body of Christ....that we should serve in newness of spirit. (Romans 7:4, 6)

For the law of the Spirit of life in Christ Jesus hath made me free from the law of sin and death. For...God...condemned sin in the flesh: that the righteousness of the law might be fulfilled in us, who walk not after the flesh, but after the Spirit.
(Romans 8:2–4)

In everything and always the Spirit and the cross are inseparable. Yes, even in heaven. The

Lamb, as it had been slain, standing in the midst of the throne had *"seven eyes, which are the seven Spirits of God sent forth into all the earth"* (Revelation 5:6). Again, *"He showed me a pure river of water of life, clear as crystal* [Is this other than the Holy Spirit?], *proceeding out of the throne of God and of the Lamb"* (Revelation 22:1). When Moses smote the rock, the water streamed out and Israel drank. When the Rock, Christ, was actually smitten, and He had taken His place as the slain Lamb on the throne of God, there flowed out from under the throne the fullness of the Holy Spirit for the whole world.

How foolish it is to pray for the fullness of the Spirit if we have not first placed ourselves under the full power of the Cross! Just think of the one hundred and twenty disciples. The crucifixion of Christ had touched, broken, and taken possession of their entire hearts. They could speak or think of nothing else, and when the Crucified One had shown them His hands and His feet, He said to them, *"Receive ye the Holy Ghost"* (John 20:22). And so also, with their hearts full of the crucified Christ, now received up into heaven, they were prepared to be filled with the Spirit. They dared to proclaim to the people, "Repent and believe in the Crucified One," and they also received the Holy Spirit.

Christ gave Himself up entirely to the Cross. The disciples also did the same. The Cross demands this also from us; it would have our entire lives. To comply with this demand requires nothing less than a powerful act of the will, for which we are unfit. It also requires a powerful act of God that will assuredly come to those who cast themselves unreservedly on Him.

THE SPIRIT

Why aren't there more men and women who can witness, in the joy of their hearts, that the Spirit of God has taken possession of them and given them new power to witness for Him? Yet more urgently arises the heart-searching question to which an answer must be given: What is it that hinders? The Father in heaven is more willing than any earthly father to give bread to His child, and yet the cry arises, "Is the Spirit restricted? Is this His work?"

Many will acknowledge that the hindrance undoubtedly lies in the fact that the church is too much under the sway of the flesh and the world. They understand too little of the heart-piercing power of the Cross of Christ. So it comes to pass that the Spirit does not have the vessels into which He can pour His fullness.

Many complain that the subject is too high or too deep for them. This is proof of how little we have appropriated and brought into practice the teaching of Paul and Christ about the Cross. I bring you a message of joy. The Spirit who is in you, in however limited a measure, is prepared to take you under His teaching, to lead you to the Cross, and, by His heavenly instruction, to make you know something of what the crucified Christ wills to do for you and in you.

But then He wants you to spend time with Him, so that He may reveal the heavenly mysteries to you. He wants to make you see how neglecting the inner chamber has hindered fellowship with Christ, the knowledge of the Cross, and the powerful operations of the Spirit. He will teach you what is meant by the denial of self, the taking up of your cross, the losing of your life, and following Him.

In spite of all that you have felt of your ignorance, and lack of spiritual insight, He is able and willing to take you under His teaching and to make known to you the secret of the spiritual life above all your expectations.

Begin at the beginning. Be faithful in the inner chamber. Thank Him that you can count on Him to meet you there. Although everything appears cold, dark, and strained, bow in silence before the loving Lord Jesus, who so longs after you. Thank the Father that He has given you the Spirit. And be assured that all you do not yet know— about the flesh, and the world, and the Cross—the Spirit of Christ, who is in you, will surely make known to you. Oh, soul, only believe that this blessing is for you! Christ belongs entirely to you. He longs to obtain full possession of you. He can and will possess you through the Holy Spirit. But for this, time is necessary. Oh, give Him time in the inner chamber every day. You can rest assured that He will fulfill His promise in you.

> *He that hath my commandments, and keepeth them, he it is that loveth me: and he that loveth me shall be loved of my Father, and I will love him, and will manifest myself to him.* (John 14:21)

Persevere, in addition to all that you ask for yourself, in prayer for your congregation, your church, your minister, for all believers, for the whole church of God, that God may strengthen them with power through His Spirit, so that Christ may dwell in their hearts by faith (Ephesians 3:16–17). Blessed time when the answer comes! Continue in prayer. The Spirit will reveal and glorify Christ and His love, Christ and His Cross, as the Lamb slain standing in the midst of the throne (Revelation 5:6).

THE CROSS AND THE FLESH

These two are deadly enemies. The cross desires to condemn and put to death the flesh. The flesh desires to cast aside and conquer the cross. Many, as they hear of the Cross as the indispensable preparation for the fullness of the Holy Spirit, will find out what is in them that must still be crucified.

We must understand that our entire nature is sentenced to death and becomes dead by the Cross, so that the new life in Christ may come to rule in us. We must obtain such an insight into the fallen condition of our nature and its enmity against God that we become willing, even desirous, to be wholly freed from it.

We must learn to say with Paul, *"In me (that is, in my flesh,) dwelleth no good thing"* (Romans 7:18). *"The* [mind of the flesh] *is enmity against God: for it is not subject to the law of God, neither indeed can be"* (Romans 8:7). It is its very essence to hate God and His holy law. This is the wonder of redemption, that Christ has borne on the cross the judgment and curse of the flesh and has forever nailed it to the cursed tree. If a man only believes God's Word about this cursed mind of the flesh, and then longs to be delivered from it, he learns to love the Cross as his deliverer from the power of the enemy.

"Our old man is crucified" with Christ (Romans 6:6), and our one hope is to receive this by faith and to hold it fast. *"They that are Christ's have crucified the flesh"* (Galatians 5:24). They have willingly declared that they will daily regard the flesh that is in them as the enemy of God, the enemy of Christ, the enemy of their soul's salvation, and will treat it as having received its deserved reward in being nailed to the cross.

This is one part of the eternal redemption that Christ has brought to us. It is not something that we can grasp with our understanding or accomplish with our strength. It is something that the Lord Jesus Himself will give us if we are willing to abide in His fellowship day by day and to receive everything from Him. It is something that the Holy Spirit will teach us. He will impart it to us as an experience and will show how He can give victory in the power of the Cross over all that is of the flesh.

THE CROSS AND THE WORLD

What the flesh is in the smallest circle of my own person, that the world is in the larger circle of mankind. The flesh and the world are two manifestations of the same god of this world who is served by both.

When the cross deals with the flesh as accursed, we at once discover what the nature and power of the world are. *"They...hated both me and my Father"* (John 15:24). The proof of this was that they crucified Christ. But Christ obtained the victory on the cross and freed us from the power of the world. And now we can say, *"God forbid that I should glory, save in the cross of our Lord Jesus Christ, by whom the world is crucified unto me, and I unto the world"* (Galatians 6:14).

Every day the Cross was to Paul a holy reality, both in what he had to suffer from the world and in the victory that the Cross constantly gave. John also wrote, *"The whole world lieth in wickedness"* (1 John 5:19). *"Who is he that overcometh the world, but he that believeth that Jesus is the Son of*

God? This is he that came by water and blood, even Jesus Christ....And it is the Spirit that beareth witness, because the Spirit is truth" (vv. 5–6).

Against the two great powers of the god of this world, God has given us two great powers from heaven, namely, the Cross and the Spirit.

Epilogue

I t is not enough that one should understand and appropriate the thought of the writer, and then rejoice because of the new insight he has obtained and the pleasure that knowledge has brought. There is something else that is of great importance. I must surrender myself to the truth so that I will be ready, with an undivided will, to immediately perform all that I will learn to be God's will.

In a book such as this, dealing with the life of prayer and hidden fellowship with God, it is indispensable that we should be prepared to receive and obey all that we see to be according to the Word and will of God. When this inner desire is lacking, knowledge only serves to make it more difficult for the heart to receive abundant life. Satan endeavors to become master of the Christian's inner chamber because he knows that if there has been unfaithfulness in prayer, then that Christian will bring little loss to Satan's kingdom. Spiritual power to lead the unsaved to the Lord or to build up the children of God will not be experienced under it. Persevering prayer, through which alone this power comes, has been lacking.

The great question has been: Will we really set ourselves to win back again the weapon of believing prayer that Satan has, in a measure, taken away from us? Let us set before ourselves the serious importance of this conflict. As far as each minister is concerned, everything depends on whether or not he is a man of prayer—one who in the inner chamber must be clothed each day with power from on high. We, in common with the church throughout the whole world, have to complain that prayer does not have the place in our service of God that it ought to have, according to the will and promise of God and according to the need of minister, congregation, and church.

The public consecration that many a believer has been led to make of himself at conferences in not an easy thing. And even when the step is taken, old custom and the power of the flesh will tend to bring it to nothing. The power of faith is not yet vigorous. It will cost strife and sacrifice to conquer the Devil in the name of Christ. Our churches are the battlefield where Satan will bring forth all his power to prevent us from becoming men of prayer, powerful in the Lord to obtain the victory in heaven and on earth. How much depends on this for ourselves, for our congregations, and for the kingdom!

Do not be surprised if I say that it is with fear and trembling, and with much prayer, that I have written what I trust will help to encourage believers in the conflict. It is with a feeling of deep unworthiness that I venture to offer myself as a guide to the inner chamber, which is the way to holiness and to fellowship with God.

Do not wonder that I have asked the Lord to give this book a place in some inner chambers, that He may assist the reader. The end result is so that as the reader sees what God's will is, he may immediately give himself up to do it. In war, everything depends on each soldier being obedient to the word of command, even though it costs him his life. In our strife with Satan, we will not conquer unless each one of us holds himself ready, even in the reading of this simple book, to say from the heart, "What God says I will do. And if I see that anything is according to His will, I will immediately receive it and act upon it." Do not wonder that I have written this message to remind believers that everything depends on the spirit of surrender to immediate obedience, according to the Word of God.

God grant that, in His great grace, this book may prove a bond of fellowship by which we may think of and help one another. I pray that we might strengthen each other for the conflict in prayer by which the Enemy may be overcome and the life of God may be gloriously revealed!